T5-ANV-247
WHS

THE NEW HUSBANDS and how to become one

Andrew J. DuBrin

THE NEW HUSBANDS and how to become one

Nelson-Hall
nh Chicago

Library of Congress Cataloging in Publication Data

DuBrin, Andrew J
The new husbands and how to become one.

Includes bibliographical references.
1. Husbands. 2. Fathers. 3. Men—Psychology.
4. Family—United States. I. Title.
HQ756.D76 301.42'7 76-15359
ISBN 0-88229-358-3

Copyright © 1976 by Andrew J. DuBrin

All rights reserved. No part of this book may be reproduced in any form without permission in writing from the publisher, except by a reviewer who wishes to quote brief passages in connection with a review written for broadcast or for inclusion in a magazine or newspaper. For information address Nelson-Hall Inc., 325 West Jackson Blvd., Chicago, Illinois 60606.

Manufactured in the United States of America

To Marcia,
who makes being a husband fun

Also by Andrew J. DuBrin

Managerial Deviance
Fundamentals of Organizational Behavior
Survival in the Sexist Jungle
The Singles Game
Women in Transition
The Practice of Managerial Psychology

Contents

Preface

Men, in their role as husbands, receive much less public attention than they deserve. Husbands are infrequently the central figure in a scientific study, novel, play, or movie. In contrast, the plight of housewives and their assimilation into the world of work has been a theme receiving constant public attention from the mid-1960s to the present. Yet the vital contribution of husbands to the liberation of their wives has been virtually ignored by social commentators. When husbands are subject to the scrutiny of a scientist, scholar, or popular writer the verdict is frequently unfavorable.

The dominating patriarch of the 1940s and earlier has been accused of gross insensitivity to the emotional well-being of his wife and children. The upward striving, career-oriented organization man of the 1950s and 1960s has been denounced as abdicating the true role of husband and father. As many husbands became disenchanted with the pursuit of high paying jobs and coping with competing demands of wives and children, they retreated into a pattern of passivity at home and in the office. A popular stereotype arose of the "lazy husband"—a person who eked out a marginal living in the world outside, then retreated home at night to guzzle beer and watch television.

Gradually a new species of husband has emerged in response to changes in society—particularly the increased emphasis upon women pursuing careers outside the home and the decreased emphasis upon materialism. Numbering about one in ten among husbands or live-in boyfriends, *the new husband* is a semiliberated, transitional male of today who attempts to juggle the demands of his wife, children, and career to the satisfaction of all three (and himself). Criticized by some as being unambitious, leisure oriented, or worse—as unmasculine—he is, nevertheless, emerging as the idealized version of the American husband-father-career person.

How does the new husband described in this book differ from the minority of men calling themselves liberated males? New husbands, in a very important sense, are moderately liberated people. Few new husbands want to entirely abandon differences in roles between males and females. They want a relationship of equality with their wives, but they do not feel victimized because society expects them to pursue worldly success. New husbands, as I define them, are looking for a more flexible definition of masculinity but they do not demand a blurring of the distinction between male and female roles.

The New Husbands describes the new variety of man who may make it possible for women's liberation, men's liberation, and even human liberation to really work. He has that special combination of toughness and tenderness, ambitiousness and contentment, and work and family orientation necessary to help make family life and monogamous relationships workable and exciting. For *old husband* readers who are curious about joining the breed of new husbands, my book offers many suggestions for bringing about the required changes in your attitudes and actions.

Acknowledgments

A substantial number of people receive my appreciation for their contribution to the production of *The New Husbands.* Bruce Merrin, my agent, provided much needed encouragement about the potential appeal of this project. K. Lois Smith turned in her usual fine performance as my manuscript typist. Dorothy J. Miller performed a variety of necessary clerical chores. About 600 males from around the United States and seven other countries wrote (and in some cases, telephoned me) in response to my classified ad, "Liberated husbands wanted for exciting research." Approximately one-half of these men completed questionnaires or were interviewed about their role as husbands. Students of mine at the Rochester Institute of Technology were also quite helpful as interviewers and interviewees about the topic of this book.

My wife Marcia has provided me with many insights into the positive aspects of male-female relationships, a large number of which have worked their way into this book. Drew and Douglas, my sons, have taught me a lot about the excitement of father-son relationships. Our daughter, Melanie, arrived several months after this manuscript was written. Nevertheless, she has given me a third opportunity to practice new concepts of fatherhood.

chapter 1

Meet the New Husbands

Gradually, unceremoniously, and without even the benefit of a formal movement, a new breed of husbands has emerged upon the North American scene. This new husband promises to replace other versions of the exemplary husband-father-breadwinner. At the turn of this century, the benevolent patriarch stood out as the ideal husband. His authority in the household was unquestioned, while his involvement in child rearing and housekeeping was limited. By the middle of the century, however, a new version of the ideal husband emerged—one who sacrificed his concern about family matters in order to climb the organizational ladder. Working long hours, traveling extensively, and often working many miles from home, his image soon became tarnished. The absentee father-husband-organization man became the target of attack of experts in child rearing. Accused of abdicating all household decision-making authority to his wife and sluffing off his child-rearing responsibilities to mother and school teachers, this kind of husband and father fell into disfavor.

By the mid-1970s the combined influence of feminists, male liberationists, hippies, and other humanists fostered a new version of the ideal husband-father-breadwinner. By then the ideal family man had cast aside the North American male obsession with getting ahead and keeping cool. The search for meaningful relationships with people became more important than the quest for power, money, and prowess. Instead of dissuading young boys from crying, the feeling-oriented adult male *encouraged* them to cry. Male liberationists joined forces with female liberationists in advocating unisexual roles in society for male and female adults and unisex toys and clothing for children. Perhaps the pendulum had swung too far in the direction away from rigidity in sex roles, pursuit of worldly success, and male insensitivity to feelings.

The *new husbands,* as I inelegantly label them, are essentially an amalgam of the good qualities of their predecessors. At their best, they are a happy combination of tenderness, toughness, concern for success in the world outside, and concern for the quality of life at home. All new husbands do not lead identical life styles; some are live-in boyfriends or common-law husbands, some are very successful in their careers, a few have modest jobs, some live in rural areas, and others live in high-rise apartments. One common thread does unite the new husbands without most of them being aware of this unifying theme. Despite the pressures toward disintegration of life today, they lead integrated, rewarding lives. Somehow, they are able to enjoy life themselves while also providing for the emotional and economic well-being of people they love. With a combination of concern for self and concern for others, they lead a kind of life that holds promise of outdistancing fads in life styles. New husbands share in decision making at home without surrendering all of their power, and they play and learn with their children without becoming children themselves.

Adam, Computer Scientist and Belly Button Comparer

Adam, age forty-one, makes about 27,000 dollars per year managing a group of computer specialists in a large company. A mathematics major in college, Adam later earned an M.B.A. to help his career along and to sharpen his intellect in the process. Asked about how his work fits into his life, Adam notes: "I'm doing much better than the average bear. Running a gung-ho operation of intelligent fellows and gals is a lot of fun. Some of the things we do for the corporation, such as setting up a system that guarantees that the right number of cans of peas will reach the customer on time, don't sound like we're saving the world. But, without us, I guess canned peas and other goodies would cost the customer even more. I've always enjoyed doing pace-setting things and our department fits into the leading edge of what's going on in business these days. I'm making a good buck and having an occasional professional thrill without any big sacrifice to my home life."

In talking about his three children, Adam comments: "What's always been important to me is the combination of silly and serious things I do with the children. Of course, what I do with my children depends upon their age at the time, but, whatever the age, it's a source of enjoyment. Making things has been fun, whether it's a set of Indian beads for the Brownies or a wooden car for the Cub Scouts. I think we've made at least ten kites that never got off the ground and three cars that wouldn't roll down hill. Watching clouds and butterflies drift by is more fun than playing organized games. Of course, we've raised all kinds of pets together, gerbils, cats, goldfish, turtles, and even an occasional garden snake. Visiting the zoo has been fun. So has drawing pictures about every conceivable instrument from pencils to pieces of barbeque charcoal.

The most hilarious thing ever was the time the three kids and I compared belly buttons. Elizabeth cried because hers turned out and ours turned in."

Adam talks favorably about his relationship with his wife: "Lorraine is getting much more out of her marriage to me than she did from her first marriage. She's a sharp businesswoman who runs a profitable gift shop. I recognize that she has as much need to unwind when she comes home from work as I do. Lorraine earns less money, but I think she has more legitimate job responsibility than I do. One bad decision and Lorraine has to cover debts with money out of her pocket. With close to one billion dollars in sales, my company can survive almost any wrong decision I make. Neither Lorraine nor I need each other to prop the other one up and that adds to our relationship. Instead of patching up each other's psyche, we're helping each other grow."

In describing how Lorraine and he handle household tasks, Adam says: "Of course with our combined incomes, we hire help for a lot of the household chores. We hire people for heavy cleaning, snow removal, gardening, and any heavy household repairs. Our two oldest children earn their allowances by doing assigned chores. My permanent assignments are preparing breakfast, keeping the family financial books, and doing the laundry. Things get done in our household without a big hassle or commotion. We try to save our energy to worry about big things in life.

"What advantages do I get out of being married? Above all, it's the sharing of experiences on a day-by-day basis. I like the female feeling of softness and gentleness that's around the house on a permanent basis. The availability of someone to talk to and listen to anytime is a tremendous fringe benefit of a good marriage. An exclusive relationship with one woman combined with the children and the house gives me a feeling of having roots. I much prefer it to my less rooted days. The marriage and family bit helps put a purpose behind whatever the hell it is you are doing in the world outside."

Derek, Elementary School Counselor and Child Toucher

Derek, age twenty-nine, earns $12,500 per year as an elementary school counselor. He reacts to his job in this way: "Few people even know what an elementary school counselor does. Some people think I'm there to dry the tears of a child who wets his or her pants at school. Others think I'm some kind of a parent surrogate who dispenses punishments when a student steps too far out of line. What matters to me the most is my perception of my job. I'm helping shape the emotional growth of very important people. The future of the world depends upon the emotional health of today's children—a fact we overlook in our penchant for concentrating our attention upon whether or not our children can duplicate the functions performed by a simple adding machine. I get feedback every day on how I'm performing in my job. When a student leaves my office with a better understanding of a problem he or she is hassling with, then I know that at least I'm doing some temporary good.

"I came up the usual route of an elementary school counselor, having first been a classroom teacher for a few years. Both my experience as a teacher and as a counselor have been helpful to me as a parent. My work schedule, following somewhat the regular school day and vacation schedule, makes it possible for me to get close to my family.

"Beth, my wife, is a food service supervisor in a nursing home. Her job is harassing at times, but the hours allow her, just like me, to function as a full-time parent. Beth deals more with facts and figures and things than I do in my job, but we have a lot to communicate about. Except for emergencies, such as illness or a particularly late evening out, we try to have our private communication session every night. For about ten minutes we just rap to each other about anything on our mind. We don't judge each other—just listen. One night I told her how much I would like to have intercourse with a counseling intern assigned to me. Instead of saying in words or by a disapproving glance that I was a prick for having such thoughts, Beth told me about how much she fantasized having sexual relations with a black chef at her nursing home.

"Mandi, our daughter, and I have a precious relationship. Although she's only a second grader, I regard her as a good friend of mine. We talk to each other a lot and we also touch each other frequently. There is nothing so tender to me as having a seven-year-old girl touch your face. We try to solve problems together like how to get a kitten down from a tree. Last time that happened Mandi suggested to me that she stand on my shoulders and reach for the cat. It worked.

"Beth, Mandi, and I share the housework. Mandi has to take out the rubbish and clean out the kitten's litter tray. Beth and I divide things up in an informal way. She more or less is in charge of feeding because she's interested in that field from a professional standpoint. We could do things more systematically, but it's often a question of who sees what needs to be done first. If I notice the TV screen is crudded up with fingerprints and potato chip grease, I apply the sponge and cleaning solvent. If I'm the first to notice the car muffler making a weird, bellowing sound, I drop by the muffler shop. Neither Beth nor I are compulsive about housekeeping chores.

"On balance, the advantages of being married outweigh the disadvantages. Of course, there is the companionship and love. Sharing financial responsibility and having your own little fortress against the outside world is also a big plus. Having sex with only one person can get a little dull sometimes but, if you're really communicating with your spouse or lover, it's no major concern."

Marv, County Legislator and Sexual Batman

Marv, age forty-six, earns $16,500 per year from his job as a county legislator and another $2,000 from a small apartment building he owns. "Working as a legislator is much more exciting than my former work as a postal supervisor. Although I worked as a public servant then, I think my contribution is more directly felt now. My new contentment with my work has made a great impact on my new home life. Many of the problems with my first two wives stemmed from my grumbling about my discontent with the postal system. I may not be as famous as the governor, but grass roots democracy is what really runs this country anyway. Right now I'm working on a rodent control program that could save a lot of people's lives.

"Elsie, my wife, is proud of being a full-time homemaker and community servant. She's into five different volunteer activities, all of which are meaningful to her. If there weren't women like Elsie around, very few things would get done in the community. She spearheaded one community chest campaign that resulted in a 25 percent increase in revenues. Elsie has one child from her first marriage, a young woman who's a college sophomore.

"As a legislator I believe in the democratic process, both at home and on the job. Elsie and I try to share jointly in every decision of consequence. To show you what I'm talking about, we recently had our house painted. The way we chose the color was for each of us to rank our color preferences one through five without telling the other person. Her first choice was blue, her second choice white, her third choice green. My first choice was grey, my second white, and my third blue. Since we both agreed on white for second choice, the house is white.

"Sharing in decision making has done many fine things for our marriage. It eliminates many problems which in turn helps our sex life. One night Elsie gave me a great compliment. She called me a sexual Batman. I asked her what she meant. Elsie said, 'Remember Marv, we said we would try to be honest with each other all the time and about almost everything. Well, I think you're pretty good at sex. But it would be stretching the truth to call you a sexual Superman, so we'll settle for Batman and let it go at that.' I'm very happy to be Batman. In my last two marriages I was no superhero in bed.

"My relationship with my children is very uncomplicated and very nice. My boy is from my first marriage, and my daughter is from my second. The boy is an automotive mechanic and we get together about once every two weeks to do something specific like attend a pro football game or auto rally. Elsie is invited and she often comes with us. My daughter is married and lives 300 miles away. We see each other a couple of times a year. There are only good feelings between us. Her husband is a nice fellow and she's leading a life that makes her happy.

"As I said, my wife is a full-time homemaker by choice, so she prefers to do most of the housework. I have the usual jobs outside the house, including keeping the cars maintained. Right now I'm paneling a sewing room in our house to make it a suitable office for Elsie. She's so busy with community affairs that she needs a nice office to operate from. She helps me with some of my mountainous correspondence when it fits her time schedule.

"The advantages of being married are none unless you get along with your wife. I get along with Elsie which leads to all kinds of advantages. If you don't get along with your wife, which I think is the case for most of my friends, marriage is worse than living in the county jail."

Scott, Writer and Househusband

Scott, age thirty-three, grossed $7,700 last year as a free-lance writer, but is looking forward to slightly increased earnings this year. "I have nothing to be defensive about. My choice is to pursue my professional writing career on as much a full-time basis as I can manage. My wife can tolerate the nine-to-five routine, but I cannot. Similarly, I'm better suited by temperament to raise our three-year-old son, Mike. It's a logical, wholesome trade-off. I manage the household and get to my writing when Mike naps or is busy in his playpen. After the dinner dishes are finished, my wife takes care of Mike until he goes to bed. That's my time for an uninterrupted hour of writing. The kitchen table is my office because we can only afford a two-bedroom apartment right now.

"When Mike begins school two years from now, I will have more time for my writing. In the interim, I'm collecting some notes for a contemplated novel about a family that is eventually destroyed because of the inefficiency in society. I tried the get-up-in-the-morning-every-weekday-until-you-become-a-robot routine for about six years. My job involved writing a corporate communications release which I would have to classify as dishonest journalism. My job was to prepare well-written, intelligent statements about things that the company was doing well. My last assignment required me to do a cover-up story of how important a recent company layoff was to the good of the organization as a whole. Since a few of my friends were laid off a week before Christmas, I felt pretty bad about the finished product.

"My life now is not highly productive from the

materialistic criteria so often used to judge success in our society, but my wife, Mike, and I are benefiting from my new life style. Carol is her own woman. She could sense that I was discontent going to work every day and she was equally discontent in the full-time homemaker role. When we finally let the obvious conclusion emerge that we should switch roles, you could see the excitement in her face. Carol has become impervious to the put-downs from relatives such as, 'Is everything okay with Scott? I notice he hasn't worked in many months. Are you worried about a little boy being raised by his Father?'

"Carol's position as a television director's assistant is low paying but psychologically rewarding. She has enough energy left over at night to enjoy Mike and me. Our relationship isn't perfect but it's viable. Every few months or so Carol gets into the materialistic, thing-possession trip. She notes that our car is falling apart and that our living room couch would not be accepted by the Salvation Army. Furthermore, she pouts about not being able to buy a new car or couch on her income. I lash back that she's becoming just like all the stereotyped people she claims not to be.

"Raising Mike on almost a full-time basis is one of the peak experiences of my life. There is no fundamental reason why a child's father shouldn't spend more time than the mother in raising a child. What I'm doing is hardly revolutionary anymore. Many magazine articles in the last few years have described househusbandry. I stay at home, but I'm also working at a worthwhile profession. Mike is an adorable kid, and I'm glad I have the chance to spend so much time with him during his formative years.

"All the complaints feminists have made in recent years about the drudgery of housework are somewhat overdrawn in my estimation. I get a small feeling of accomplishment whenever the house looks clean or I have prepared a nutritious, well-received meal. Perhaps the best aspect of housework is that it gives you something to do with your hands while you are thinking about something else. I get most of my ideas for articles when I'm doing manual chores like washing dishes or mopping the floor.

"For me, the unique advantage of being married is that it enables me to lead the life style I prefer. Of course, there is also the love and companionship from my wife and child and the feeling that these relationships will last. Being a househusband and writer could only work if you and your wife are emotionally close."

Frank, Company President and Hair Stylist

Frank, age thirty-six, is black and earns $33,000 per year as the president of Precision Components, Inc., a small company providing electronic parts for industrial machinery. Asked about his work, Frank comments, "Face it, this is where the action is in America. Running your own show is the American Dream for whites and blacks alike. My talent is in selling, not in making parts or managing the books. I leave those arduous chores to my colleagues who are more talented in those areas than I. My company was founded on the basis of my ability to sell. A couple of major companies in the area originally placed orders with us as part of the movement to help black enterprise along. Now we could survive quite nicely without their orders. I'm a black nationalist and proud of it. My success in business and the stature it gives me in the community has had a tremendous positive impact upon my marriage.

"My wife, Marylee, comes from the bottom of the barrel economically. In her family, the mother made all the decisions and kept the family glued together through hard times. I am Mr. Big in my family and it suits my wife and two girls just fine. I care for them and relate to them as equals on the home front, but I am still a very important, powerful person in their eyes. My mother-in-law thanks me monthly for being so great to her daughter.

"Marylee works for fun and very little profit as a part-time receptionist in a health spa. Her good looks and charming manner are used to good advantage in such a job. Even more important, Marylee is much happier since she took this job two years ago. It seems to give her just enough change of pace from her home responsibilities to keep her life interesting. Should she want to increase the amount of time she spends working, that would be fine with me. Marylee is a mature person who would be able to recognize what was happening if she began to slice up her life too thinly. So far she keeps a fine balance between work inside the home and outside the home.

"Philosophically, Marylee and I get along well on every issue but one. She feels I am too hung up on Black Awareness, while I feel that she is becoming too middle-class white in her attitudes and values. She wants us to move to a virtually all-white suburb just because we can afford it. I want to remain in the highest income black neighborhood. We go round and round on this issue every once in a while and I don't know if it will ever be resolved. No good compromise comes to mind.

"I'm not a big contributor to running the household except for small mechanical repairs that we don't contract outside for. But I have one speciality that I'm particularly proud of. Everybody has some silly secret dream to do something for a living completely outside the mainstream of what he might actually be doing for a living. Well, I would like to be a woman's hair stylist. I've got the perfect opportunity at home. Tracy and Jill, my seven-year-old twins, and Marylee all get their hair styled by Mr. Frank of Paris. Since Marylee won't consent to Afro's, the challenge is all the bigger and I love it. Saturday afternoon around five is time for the appointment with Mr. Frank unless a crisis develops. Once I fractured my left arm skiing, but it resulted in only one missed appointment. I simply styled with one arm in a cast, and then used a sling for a couple of months.

"You ask me the advantages of being a husband? My impressions are related to my own experiences. Aside from the feeling of being needed by a few people, it's my way of saying to the world 'Look, I've arrived. I'm a powerful person both at work and at home. I can keep three people I love happy with a minimum of tromping on each other's independence.' Until some brilliant sociologist comes up with a better idea, the family is still the best modular unit for building a society."

Tony, Architect and Pillow Fluffer

Tony, age twenty-seven, earns $19,500 as an architect for commercial buildings. Gwyn, age twenty-three, a high school art teacher, and he share a two-bedroom town house. Tony reflects, "My work as an architect is my special thing. I recently read, in a book about industrial psychology, something to the effect that an architect is both an artist and a scientist. In order to do well as an architect a person must act like a businessman, lawyer, artist, engineer, and advertising man. In addition, he's supposed to have the back-up skills of an author, journalist, educator, and psychiatrist. After being in the field a few years, I understand the truth in that statement. I'm proud to be an architect. One unexpected fringe benefit is that it helps my relationship with Gwyn. By both being creative people we can understand each other much better than if one of us were creative and the other were not. If I can't achieve what I want in one of my designs, I get emotionally down and Gwyn can understand. If Gwyn can't bring out the creativity in her students that she wants, or can't put the right expression into one of her own paintings, she too gets down. We also share our 'ups.'

"Gwyn and I have more of an open relationship than any couple we know. Maybe our not being married has helped us to escape the feeling of entrapment that grabs so many people. I'll explain what being open means to us in our relationship. Every once in a while Gwyn or I will take off on a Sunday to do something on our own. And this taking off can happen the Sunday after we had a great thing going the Saturday night before. It is not related to anger or problems. When one of us leaves on a Sunday for a day off from the other, it automatically gives the other person a day off also.

"Let's say I took the day off to watch the stock car races or just go fishing. When I come home, Gwyn doesn't grill me about where I've been or try to determine if I've been spending time with a woman. If I want to spend time with a woman on my day off it would hurt Gwyn's feelings, but she wouldn't regard it as a crisis in our relationship. I assume my feelings would be hurt if Gwyn spent time with a man on her day off, but it isn't something I have given much thought to. Our need is to give each other a little breathing room here and there. Neither of us is longing for additional companionship. We have a solid thing going with each other.

"Children just don't fit into our plans right now. I assume if someday we do try to have children we would marry each other, but it just isn't a topic of concern right now. Our life style is fine for the present.

"When you live with someone and you both work, it would be bizarre not to share household tasks. We work on total tasks. For instance, keeping up the living room and bathrooms is my job. Gwyn irons, washes, and cooks weekday dinners. I'm in charge of breakfast plus the

Saturday and Sunday night dinners. I can cook or pay for dinner in a restaurant. Don't think our relationship is all that mechanistic. Gwyn has a terrific sense of humor. It was her idea that whoever gets out of bed last must make the bed. I prefer to sleep late and Gwyn has to leave earlier for work than I do. So it's usually my responsibility. Besides, she tells me I am much more of a virtuoso in fluffing the pillows than she is.

"The advantages of being a live-in boyfriend are all the advantages of being married without some of the relationship-crushing aspects of marriage. Even though it may in reality be a myth, we feel less confined than most married people. Living with a groove like Gwyn has unique advantages over living with an ordinary woman. I have a constant source of emotional support if I need it, but I don't have that cloying dependency if I don't want it for the moment. When either Gwyn or I sense that one of us doesn't need warmth or attention from the other at the moment, we back off.

"A few times friends and relatives have suggested that the reason we are not married is that we fear making a commitment to each other. It's not true; we have a strong commitment to each other but we work with our relationship a day at a time. Every month our employers deduct money from our paychecks to pay for Social Security and pensions. That's enough concern about forty years from now for me. I don't like the idea of a marriage contract being used as a form of retirement planning. Gwyn and I agree wholeheartedly on one thing. What really counts in a relationship is how things are going for the present. For us the present is beautiful."

chapter 2

Do You Think Like a New Husband?

Before reading more about new husbands (and receiving suggestions on how to become one if you are not already there and want to convert), it is important to compare your thinking with that of new husbands. For this purpose, I have prepared the New Husband Rating Scale which provides you with the opportunity to classify yourself as belonging to one of three different categories of husbands. More will be said about the specifics of these categories later.

One cautionary note should be kept in mind before taking this scale. The situation a man finds himself in can influence whether or not he behaves as a new husband. For instance, Len might enjoy participating fully in child rearing but might be repelled by the prospects of sharing work assignments in the kitchen. Tim might fully participate in all aspects of fatherhood—including helping his teen-age daughter select clothing for herself. He might enjoy sewing on buttons while his wife is outside mowing the lawn and pruning trees. Yet Tim is a staunch "old husband" in his attitudes toward his wife working outside the home. He feels that a woman has enough to do as manager of the home without taking on the additional burden of a job in the world outside.

Can women also take this scale? Decidedly yes. Although only a handful of lesbians see themselves as being "husbands" in a relationship with another person, most women have strong attitudes about relationships between males and females. All questions ask for your attitudes or opinions about a particular situation. You do not have to belong to a particular category of people in order to have attitudes about how they should best act in a given situation. For instance, you might have an attitude about the following situation which deals with tennis customs without yourself being a professional tennis player.

	Mostly Agree	Mostly Disagree
After a man wins a long, hard-fought match against another man in a tennis tournament, he should hug him.	______	______

On to the New Husband Rating Scale. Simply read each question and check in the appropriate space whether you "mostly agree" or "mostly disagree." Answer each question even if you are silently muttering, "I hate to answer *mostly agree* or *mostly disagree,* when my real answer is *it depends upon the situation.*"

How honestly should you answer these questions? Anybody intelligent enough to read this book is intelligent enough to place himself or herself in a favorable light on this scale. However, without an honest attempt at candor on your part you are unlikely to learn anything about yourself of value to you in your relationship with your spouse or live-in boyfriend or girlfriend.

The New Husband Scale

	Mostly Agree	Mostly Disagree
1. A husband and wife should have separate checking accounts.	______	______
2. A man who really loved a woman would be willing to change his name to her last name.	______	______
3. A husband should only talk to his wife about his work under unusual circumstances.	______	______
4. A husband and wife do not necessarily have to take vacations together.	______	______
5. A wife should ask for her husband's approval before changing her hair length.	______	______
6. A man and woman should take turns cleaning up after the mess a baby sometimes makes at the dinner table.	______	______
7. When a woman marries a man equal to her in height, she should be careful to wear flat shoes when they are together.	______	______
8. A man should only be required to do housework in emergency situations.	______	______
9. A husband has every right to know where his wife is at all times (with exceptions for emergencies).	______	______
10. A husband should talk about his wife's career to his friends.	______	______

	Mostly Agree	Mostly Disagree
11. Assuming a baby is bottle fed, the man and woman should take turns with the early morning feeding.	______	______
12. When a woman enters the family business, she should never be given a job of equal or higher rank than her husband.	______	______
13. More men should be encouraged to give full-time homemaking a try.	______	______
14. A father should become actively involved in child rearing even before his children reach school age.	______	______
15. When a wife says to her husband at 7 P.M., "I'll be home around midnight," he should not ask "Where are you going?"	______	______
16. A father with a son and daughter should devote an equal amount of time and emotional energy to both.	______	______
17. A father should only change a baby's diaper if the mother is ill or otherwise unavailable.	______	______
18. Even when a wife does not work outside the home, a husband should do some of the household chores.	______	______
19. Pleasing the man is the most important aspect of sex between husband and wife.	______	______

	Mostly Agree	Mostly Disagree
20. A husband should be willing to switch fields if his wife considers his present line of work unethical.	______	______
21. It might be a good idea for a mother to spend an entire weekend alone with her adolescent son.	______	______
22. If a husband has a den, his wife should also have one.	______	______
23. A husband should not object if his wife has lunch with a mutual male friend.	______	______
24. Men should be granted paternity leave by their employers so they can stay home for a few months to tend a newborn child.	______	______
25. A woman who loved her husband would have no need to work outside the home.	______	______
26. A husband should almost never cry in front of his wife.	______	______
27. A man who lets his wife make big decisions in the family automatically surrenders some of his masculinity.	______	______
28. It might be a good idea for a father to spend an entire weekend alone with his adolescent daughter.	______	______

	Mostly Agree	Mostly Disagree
29. Mothers should help children with liberal arts and social studies subjects; fathers should help them with math and physical sciences.	_______	_______
30. A man who lets a woman support him while he stays home and takes care of the house has something wrong with his mentality.	_______	_______
31. Cleaning the bathroom is strictly "woman's work."	_______	_______
32. A husband who is planning an affair should inform his wife so that she can plan an equal opportunity for herself.	_______	_______
33. A husband should not become upset if his wife sorts through his wallet and attache case while he is sleeping.	_______	_______
34. A husband has the right to spank his wife if she has an extramarital affair.	_______	_______
35. When a woman marries she should keep her name and not assume her husband's last name.	_______	_______
36. Cleaning the garage is strictly "man's work."	_______	_______
37. It spells trouble for a marriage when a wife earns more money than her husband.	_______	_______

	Mostly Agree	Mostly Disagree
38. A father should allow himself to cry in front of his children, on occasion.	______	______
39. A husband should be willing to pay his wife's tuition for law school, assuming he can raise the money.	______	______
40. The man of the house should automatically be placed in charge of family finances.	______	______

Calculating Your Score

Every question among the forty you have just answered is worth one, two, three, or four points toward your new husband rating. Follow the straightforward scoring key presented next to arrive at a total score on the New Husband Rating Scale. Record your score value in the space provided after each question. For example, if you answered the first question "mostly agree," you would receive one point toward your new husband score. If you answered "mostly disagree," you would receive zero points for that question.

Question Number:	**Enter your score for each question in this column**
1. Mostly agree is worth 1 point.	______
2. Mostly agree is worth 4 points.	______
3. Mostly disagree is worth 1 point.	______
4. Mostly agree is worth 2 points.	______
5. Mostly disagree is worth 1 point.	______

6. Mostly agree is worth 3 points. ______
7. Mostly disagree is worth 1 point. ______
8. Mostly disagree is worth 3 points. ______
9. Mostly disagree is worth 1 point. ______
10. Mostly agree is worth 1 point. ______
11. Mostly agree is worth 2 points. ______
12. Mostly disagree is worth 3 points. ______
13. Mostly agree is worth 3 points. ______
14. Mostly agree is worth 2 points. ______
15. Mostly agree is worth 3 points. ______
16. Mostly agree is worth 1 point. ______
17. Mostly disagree is worth 4 points. ______
18. Mostly agree is worth 4 points. ______
19. Mostly disagree is worth 4 points. ______
20. Mostly agree is worth 3 points. ______
21. Mostly agree is worth 1 point. ______
22. Mostly agree is worth 1 point. ______
23. Mostly agree is worth 2 points ______
24. Mostly agree is worth 4 points. ______
25. Mostly disagree is worth 4 points. ______
26. Mostly disagree is worth 4 points. ______
27. Mostly disagree is worth 3 points. ______
28. Mostly agree is worth 2 points. ______
29. Mostly disagree is worth 3 points. ______
30. Mostly disagree is worth 3 points. ______
31. Mostly disagree is worth 2 points. ______
32. Mostly agree is worth 3 points. ______
33. Mostly agree is worth 3 points. ______
34. Mostly disagree is worth 2 points. ______
35. Mostly agree is worth 4 points. ______
36. Mostly disagree is worth 2 points. ______
37. Mostly disagree is worth 2 points. ______
38. Mostly agree is worth 3 points. ______
39. Mostly agree is worth 1 point. ______
40. Mostly disagree is worth 4 points. ______

Add your scores for each question to arrive at your *total score.* If your answer to any question is the opposite of the answer in the key (for example, agree in place of disagree) your score for that question is 0. _______

Interpretation of Scores

Assuming you answered the New Husband Scale with as much candor as possible, and also assuming that you have a conscious awareness of your attitudes about most of the situations described in the scale, your score can be interpreted with reasonable accuracy. An important precaution in interpreting your score is to recognize that this scale is not foolproof. Although accepted methods of attitude scale construction underlie the New Husband Scale, it does not have the full scientific status of a standardized psychological test. The score you receive (and the category in which it places you) should be interpreted as an approximate categorization of your thinking about the most appropriate actions and attitudes for a husband-father-career person. For instance, a few people who score as *new husbands* or *totally liberated husbands* on this scale might actually behave as *old husbands* at home.

Old Husband. Scores of 50 or under suggest that you think like an old-fashioned, traditional husband. You perhaps believe that the "woman's place is in the home," that "the man should wear the pants in the family," and that child rearing is essentially woman's work. The lower your score, the more extreme your attitudes are likely to be in these directions. Extremely low scorers shun the women's liberation movement and perceive men who do housework as "pansies." In order for you to have peaceful relations at home, it is important that your wife represent the "nice old-fashioned girl." Changes in the role of men and women are probably passing you by—a fact that may not disturb you.

Assume that you are concerned about being an extreme *old husband* and you want to change. A starting point would be a careful reading of this book with a particular emphasis upon the final chapter. Above all, you need sensitizing to the ways in which you are acting and thinking like an old husband. Perhaps your wife and children can help bring old-husband attitudes and practices to your attention.

New Husband. Unlike most rating scales with which you are probably familiar, the highest score on this scale does not necessarily mean the *best* score. A score in the medium range of the scale (51–89 points) suggests that you think like a new husband—that is, a well-integrated person who is proud of being male and yet is also sensitive to the emotional well-being of his wife or girlfriend and children. You do what you can to be an involved, active father and husband but in the process you do not sacrifice your own career growth potential or your personal interests outside of women and children. Perhaps you are a *real man,* but not necessarily a *he-man* or *man's man.* You enjoy the company of men but you also enjoy the company of women and children. From my standpoint, you do not require any overall changes in your attitudes toward women, children, or the relationship of your career to the family's welfare. Stay the way you are and don't be defensive or apologetic about yourself.

Totally Liberated Husband. Extremely high scores on the scale (those of 90 or over) generally indicate that you are a male who wants to be free of role definitions about what a male should or should not do. You resent the idea that there should be separate father or mother roles. You feel that both males and females need to be liberated from being pushed into sex-linked roles by society. *Totally liberated husbands* like you tend to feel that the John Wayne image of the ideal American male has done more harm than good to society. As a countermaneuver to the roles society selects for males and females, you, as a totally liberated husband, encourage your boys to play with dolls and your daughters to play with toy automobiles. If you scored 100 on the New Husband Scale, you would probably enjoy being a full-time househusband. As several totally liberated husbands have told me, "The only purely female role in society is to bear children and breast-feed them. The only purely male role is to provide the necessary sperm for fertilization. All the rest is imposed by society."

My opinion is that the *totally liberated husband* has found the right pendulum but he has let it take him too far. Without some delineation between male and female behavior in society the result can only be confusion about sex identification and the imposition of bisexuality upon children. (Bisexuality, of course, is not inherently bad, but young people should at least be given a chance at becoming heterosexual—a topic which I shall discuss in a later chapter.) Totally liberated husbands sometimes overcompensate in the direction of squelching other people's concern for material success. In their rightful concern that too many men have been pushed toward achieving goals they do not care about (such as climbing the organizational ladder), they have begun to foster the notion that concern with career success is inherently undesirable.

An Evening of Provocative Dialogue

Now that you have completed the scale yourself, I would strongly recommend that your spouse, boyfriend, or girlfriend take the New Husband Scale. Compare your responses with respect to both total scores and your answers and reactions to particular items. Although more research evidence is needed on the topic, it appears that couples who score too far apart on the scale are in urgent need of some heavy dialogue. Suppose, for example, that the woman scores 92, and the man scores 10 on the scale. It suggests that she feels males and females should handle life's responsibilities on a completely sharing, cooperative, and equal basis. He, in contrast, believes strongly that a woman's activities should follow the *Kinder, Kirche, Kuche* (children, church, and kitchen) philosophy espoused by the Nazis of the World War II era.

Assuming the two of you have disagreements over a host of minor matters, the underlying reason may be your opposing attitudes on the proper roles of the male and female relationship. Even if your total scores are closer—suggesting good agreement between the two of you on male and female roles—a discussion of specific items could be fruitful. To take one of many examples, suppose the man mostly agrees that "A man who lets his wife make big decisions in the family, automatically surrenders some of his masculinity," and the woman mostly disagrees. The ensuing discussion is virtually guaranteed to make for an evening of provocative dialogue.

chapter 3

The Sharing Pattern

Central to the life style of the new husband is an emphasis upon the sharing of life's major and minor responsibilities between him and his wife. Unlike the proverbial henpecked, dominated husband, the new husband is not badgered into playing an active part inside the home; he does so voluntarily. The new husband also stands in sharp contrast to the powerful figure who relegates all housekeeping chores to his wife and children, and yet attempts to retain exclusive responsibility for making all major decisions that relate to the home.

The new husband operates on the premise that "I'm only one member of a team called a family. I believe in teamwork on the job, on the playing field, and at home." His submissive, Casper Milquetoast counterpart says to himself, "I hate sharing power with the old lady, but if it keeps her off my back, I'll do it." In further contrast, the traditional-minded patriarch believes, "God damnit, I make all (or most) of the money around here; let my wife and kids do all the crud that needs doing around the house. If I wanted to do housework I would have looked for a job as a butler."

Convincing evidence that the sharing pattern is becoming the preferred mode of husbandhood can be gleaned from the results of a recent Roper poll sponsored by Virginia Slims. Over 60 percent of the women under thirty expressed a preference for a spouse who could be relied upon to share in all aspects of running a household and raising a family. As a woman student of mine said in a class discussion: "I don't want to be married to a bully or a twerp either. The fellow I'm living with right now is a very close friend of mine. We treat each other as equals but I respect his opinion when we disagree. I suspect we will get married in a few years. I'll take his name but that won't imply that I'm a slave or that he will have to spend the rest of his life working for me."

Decision Making

A bold prediction Betty Yorburg makes in *The Changing Family* is that eventually no one person will be the dominant figure in the household. All important decisions will be shared. She writes: "The head of the household, as concept and as fact, will disappear. Parents will defer to and learn from children if the occasion suggests, as they defer to and learn from each other. There will be more experimentation, more choice, and more tolerance of individual, subcultural, and cultural differences in family role concepts and behavior."[1]

An overwhelming theme from the comments made by the new husbands in my research was the idea of sharing decision making with their wives. Sharing can mean that virtually all decisions are made jointly, or that decisions to be made are divided into "his and hers." One wag pointed out, "Right now my wife makes 90 percent of all the decisions around the house. Now thanks to women's lib, she wants 50 percent of my 10 percent." Despite the protests of an occasional dominated husband like this man, most new husbands see the sharing of decision as contributing to a comfortable and natural life together.

Ken, a forty-two-year-old training director, writes, "Decision making in our household works more smoothly than it does in my company. Elsa (his wife) decides about the menus, the children's clothing, and her clothing. I make decisions on savings allocations, my own involvement and degree of involvement in outside activities, and on most of the money considerations and allocations. However, most of the family decisions like housing, household decor, life insurance, and vacations are compromises with both having input and both living with decisions made that way, with either one of us saying 'I told you so' only occasionally." A rabid believer in egalitarian marriages might feel that the man in this situation has too much control over finances. What must not be overlooked is that each couple should work out for themselves the distribution of decision-making power within the family that works best for them. In this situation Ken might have more of a preference and aptitude for financial management than does Elsa.

Dr. Tom Plough, a college administrator, describes the decisions typically made by his wife, currently a full-time homemaker: "Bedtime, overnights (for the children), what the children should eat, priority on internal repairs or refurbishing, reading material for the boys, toys for them, choice of schools—in consultation with me." Tom typically makes these kinds of decisions: "Nature of weekend activities, general charge account limits, major expenditures (in consultation with his wife), general budget (no limitations on food or clothing—she decides what is needed and can buy it)." Obviously Tom and his wife trust each other's judgment enough so that this kind of dividing up of the household decision making can work.

Sumner E. Bullock, a steel construction estimator-salesman from Reseda, California, represents the viewpoint of the totally liberated husband with respect to decision making in the home: "We have virtually no he or she decisions. All decisions affecting home, business, and children, with very few occasional exceptions, are made after discussion by the both of us. We generally reach agreement on most of these type decisions." One reason this arrangement may work well for the Bullocks is the nature of his wife's occupation, which Sumner lists as "homemaker and radical feminist."

Household Tasks

New husbands are busy little housekeepers and many are quite proud of that fact. An author, who is a new husband type, recently told the book review editor of a national television show, "One of my exclusive tasks in our household is ironing. I iron my shirts, handkerchiefs, and whatever it is of my wife's that requires ironing. Her tennis outfits made out of delicate, all-synthetic fabrics represent the biggest challenge. My wife frankly admits that I have more skill in ironing than she does. No, I don't find it incongruous that my wife talks to me or watches television while I'm ironing. There are times when I'm reading or relaxing while she is busy with some household task."

My research with new husbands suggests that most of them devote about eight hours a week to household chores even when their wives are not employed outside the home. A survey of some 1,300 families in the central New York State area reported by Dr. Kathryn Walker several years ago provides corroborative information. She noted that husbands spent 1.6 hours daily with child-rearing and housekeeping activities. What kinds of tasks new husbands perform is perhaps more crucial than how much time they spend. A dynamo of a housekeeper might be able to get twice as much accomplished in the same amount of time as his more lethargic male counterpart in another household. Next, seven new husbands with working wives mention the nature of their regular housekeeping responsibilities.

Charles D. Curran, a reimbursement supervisor: "Washing the dishes, emptying trash, cleaning, and generally sharing the load. Sometimes cooking dinner. Shopping for groceries."

William B. A. Culp, Jr., a county government department head: "Cleaning house, doing the dishes, garden work, painting, yard work, light cooking and laundry. (Each of these tasks is done as my turn comes up in the cooperative, four adults and one child, in which we live.)"

Andrew P. Davis, an operations coordinator for a chain of Mexican restaurants: "Laundry every other week, one-half of the dishes, all the vacuuming, taking garbage out, one-half of the grocery shopping, and cleaning the bathroom."

Paul H. Finch, social worker: "Cooking breakfast, some regular cleaning as well as cleaning whatever my wife needs done at the time, and most of the outdoor work such as watering. In general, the work is divided according to our interests, abilities, and availability."

Stephen M. Thaxton, resource teacher at a children's center: "Cleaning, ironing, washing, cooking, vacuuming, dusting, dishes, and cleaning the oven."

An anonymous business analyst-accountant: "Household chores such as dusting, mopping, vacuuming, painting, making repairs, and occasionally preparing breakfast."

Gary Gordon, owner and manager of "Gary's Books and Hobbies": "Cooking—90 percent of the meals prepared at home, dishwashing—10 percent, garbage removal—90 percent, insect control—50 percent, clothes washing and shopping—5 percent each. All my figures are approximate."

New husbands whose wives are full-time homemakers quite often also contribute to housekeeping. One such husband is Glenn B. Gamble, a Christian minister. His responsibilities are: "Vegetable gardening, helping prepare foods for canning and for the food freezer, maintenance of house grounds, sometimes cooking a meal, and garbage disposal. In general, whatever is needed and whenever it's needed."

Sharing of household tasks works best when each person has total responsibility for a given task—either permanently or for a period of time agreed upon in advance. The least workable system of sharing for most people is one whereby one spouse attempts to help out the other on an informal, spontaneous basis. For instance, holding a dustpan for somebody is much less helpful than agreeing to take turns sweeping. Called *total task responsibility,* I describe this system in my book, *Survival in the Sexist Jungle:*

> Based upon considerable research evidence with people working in industry, this approach suggests that husband and wife have total responsibility for separate housekeeping chores. For instance, the husband might have total responsibility for the family room, basement, garage, and car maintenance. His task would be to perform any function *he thought* necessary to keep the family room, basement, garage, and cars in proper shape. Your liberated husband would

mop, dust, wax, paint, repair, purchase equipment, or buy new furniture when he thought these activities needed doing. Nagging by the spouse about when and how to perform these tasks is discouraged, if not forbidden. Couples not using total task responsibility often end up bickering about picayune topics: "I've dusted the family room, but you didn't mop yet, and it looks terrible."[2]

Child Raising

"It's beyond my comprehension why Bert ever wanted children. All he does for them on a regular basis is to pay bills. His only activity with them is having an occasional game of catch out on the front lawn. We really had a blowup last Saturday afternoon. It was a rainy day and I had a lot of errands that needed doing. I left the house, leaving Bert and the two children behind. When I came home two hours later, Dale, the two-year-old, had cigarette butts clenched in his hand and was grinding them into the white carpeting. Jennie, the four-year-old, was actually walking across her father's stomach while he was napping on the living room couch.

"When my husband and I argue about his approach to child rearing he tells me that his work is so demanding that he has very little energy left over to play with the children. He also tells me that when the children get older, it will be more natural for him to spend time with them. My argument is that by that time it will be too late. Dale and Jennie won't need him by then."

Complaints such as these are uttered by thousands of women married to *old husbands*—those who view child raising as essentially a woman's responsibility. New husbands, in contrast, regard raising children as a source of pleasure, some frustration, and challenge to be shared on an approximately equal basis with their wives. A growing number of new husbands have sought and won custody of their children upon divorce. In recent years a handful of bachelors with a new husband orientation toward life have adopted children. An aggressive, positive approach to raising children is so crucial to the new husband life style that it will be given separate attention in a later chapter. For now, the thoughts of a few men about their relationship with their children will be sampled to illustrate the depth of their involvement in child rearing. New husbands characteristically spend ten or more hours a week of productive, involved time with their child or children.

Alan E. Kinney, distribution engineer in a public utility and father of two preschool children, estimates that he spends about twenty-four hours a week in child rearing. Alan both does child-oriented activities with his children and includes them in some of his chores around the house. Says Kinney, "The things I do with my children include general roughhousing, structured play such as games, trips to the zoo, going to exhibits, trips to the ice cream parlor, yard work, occasional story reading, and helping with the baths."

Boyd, a scientist, has one child—a male second grader upon whom he has a profound influence. He reflects, "My time with Otis is very precious to me. I have some very definite ideas about father-child relationships and I practice them with Otis. It makes much more sense to share an activity with a child than to tell him he should do it for his own welfare. For instance, I got involved in the Suzuki method of teaching children how to play the violin. In essence, it means that the father and child learn to play together. I don't consider myself a natural talent at things musical, but I've learned a lot. More important than the whole experience of Otis learning to play the violin with me is that it has brought us even closer together.

"I'll give you another example of how my ideas on raising a child differ from those of most people. A big problem I see with most middle-class children is that they have a limited perspective of how different people live. I think the idea of taking your child for a drive through the slums twice a year really doesn't work. The child just gapes out the car window as if he were visiting a zoo or seeing a movie. My approach has been to take Otis regularly to diners in the poorest section of town. This way he gets to feel comfortable with old people, working people, and even society's castoffs.

"I try to stop Otis from caring so much about receiving expensive gifts and owning things but I recognize it's a losing battle in this society. If you push too hard in that direction, your child runs the danger of being seen as an oddball by friends and relatives. I'm willing to make some concessions to the fact that you can't re-create society to fit in with your ideas about raising children."

Holden, an attorney from Bay City, Michigan, is a father of twins, and the husband of a full-time college student. He describes his major activities with his children as "Roughhousing, reading, helping in toilet training (when it was needed), conversing with them (particularly at bedtime), playing ball, preparing them for bed, shopping, fishing from the shore, visits to local parks and playgrounds, trips to the car wash, and so on.

"Nevertheless, I think you are asking the wrong question. A listing of activities that I do with Pam and Gregory misses the major point. The time I spend with Pam and Greg is time spent with two little people with whom I am deeply emotionally involved. What we do is incidental to the fact that we are three people sharing experiences. Please don't misinterpret my comments to mean that time spent with my children is all the intellectual stimulation I require. My work as an attorney and my reading give me intellectual stimulation of a professional nature. Time spent with children is another form of mental stimulation, and it's sometimes more demanding than my work. I used to develop a feeling of frustration when one of the twins would ask a question like 'Dad, how come ants don't fall down when they walk upside down?' It's a lot easier to explain to a client why they can't change their depreciation schedule on an investment property."

Friends

"Honey, that was Mitchell on the phone. He's so excited he can hardly contain himself. As we saw on TV last night, Mitch has been elected to the town council. It's a big day for him and he has to share the news with somebody. I know his wife doesn't give a damn about his political activities; that's one of the reasons he wants to talk to us. I told him to come right over. But I won't be able to give him much time because I have a 9 P.M. match at the tennis club. I assume that's okay with you. Mitch and you are as close as he and I."

No, the recipient of the above phone call is not setting his wife up for possible sexual contact with Mitch. He is merely demonstrating by his actions that a new husband and his wife *share* friends. Mitchell recognizes that both this new husband and his wife are his friends (and therefore receptive to listening to his good fortune). In contrast, an *old husband* would only feel comfortable in a situation whereby Mitchell came over to the house accompanied by his own wife—who would then represent the appropriate companion for the *old husband's* wife.

A totally liberated husband often has an even more progressive view than does the new husband about sharing friends. Asked how he or his wife would feel if one or the other had an affair with a shared friend, Todd commented:

"It has happened already. Mona and our mutual friend Rick got on pretty well with each other. Quite often when Rick was over, Mona spent a lot of time in private conversation with him. One night after dinner, Mona told me she had something important to talk about. She told me, 'Todd, as you know Rick and I have become pretty close. We decided that we ought to see how good we were for each other physically. I spent an afternoon with him and we did have sexual relations. It was fine, I felt good, but I still care about you and don't want this to affect our relationship. Rick and I may or may not have a sexual encounter again in the future.'

"My thoughts were that Mona must have had a strong need for experimentation which is only natural. For me to put her down or judge her for having done a perfectly natural act would have been immature on my part. Rick and I can still be good friends. In some ways I feel closer to him now because he has helped a person I love—Mona—satisfy her sexual curiosity."

Mona and Todd have since split up. Mona and Rick are now living together while Todd is on his own and unattached at the moment. Considering that one out of five marriages now terminates in divorce (the true figure despite the repeated misinterpretation of divorce statistics claiming that about half of the marriages wind up in divorce), Todd and Mona's sharing of their friend cannot necessarily be cited as the reason for the downfall of their relationship. Nevertheless, sharing friends on a sexual level would probably weaken most relationships.

Breadwinning

"My earnings as a real estate broker would be enough to support my wife and three children. We wouldn't live elegantly, but we would be comfortable. However, if I were the person responsible for making all the money,

Letty and I would probably wind up in the same battles that plague so many marriages. Letty would soon be objecting to my handing her an allowance every month or week to pay household bills. If she managed the books, I would probably get a little miffed that she was managing the money that I was earning and she was in fact telling me how much I could spend on such and such. Letty only earns half as much as I do, but her financial contribution to the family budget is very welcome. She has taken on the responsibility of paying for remodeling of the house and buying a second car in addition to paying for food and her clothing.

"Because Letty now works outside the home, she has more respect for work. She realizes how hard it is to keep hustling all the time to hold a job or earn a salary increase. I have always done my share of housework, even before Letty worked. Now she has taken her turn in both contributing to the family income in addition to taking the major responsibility for housekeeping. Our whole life seems more balanced now."

A curious relationship seems to exist between the life style of a husband and the differential between his income and his wife's. Although there are many exceptions to this general principle, it appears that the more traditional husbands tend to earn much more than their wives. For instance, a traditional husband who is an executive might earn $35,000 a year while his wife earns $8,000 as a retail store clerk. In general, there appears to be a smaller differential between the income of new husbands and their wives. One of many examples is Ned, a social worker who earns $14,400 while his wife earns $11,000 as a school teacher. Totally liberated husbands are more often those who earn an income equivalent to or less than that of their wife.

One such liberated husband is William J. Brindle, a

sociologist from Rochester, New York, whose wife is a college professor, teaching political science. Brindle contends that a male who prefers his wife to turn down a promotion in order that she have less visible success than he loses more than money or prestige: "He foregoes the joy and satisfaction of participating in the success of a loved one." Brindle also noted in an article he wrote for a local newspaper, "Recently one of my students asked a question she assumed would challenge this very argument. 'Yes,' she said, 'but would you like to be married to a woman who was brighter and made more money than you do?' My answer then and now is, 'I am, and I wish she did.'" Assuming Professor Brindle can predict his own reactions to a hypothetical situation, it can be assumed he will accept with equanimity the day his wife outdistances him in earnings.

Wendell, a professor of English literature married to a physician, falls somewhere on the border line between being a new husband and a totally liberated husband. The income differential between Wendell and his wife is $20,000 per year in her favor (if you accept the notion that earning more income than another individual is a more *favorable* position). Wendell is unperturbed by this difference in income between him and his wife.

"The fact that you ask me such a question suggests that it might be a conflict area for you in male-female relationships. If society deems it a more economically valuable skill to tend to the physiological and anatomical misfortunes of people than to provide for their intellectual stimulation, I will accept the verdict. An individual who can help the young generation interpret the world about them through literature is seen as less economically dear than a person who can help others direct a newborn baby through the birth canal. A strange ordering of priorities from my vantage point as a professor of English literature, but I am not bitter because my wife can capitalize upon this inequity. Besides, I enjoy the world travel that my wife's luxurious income enables us to pursue."

Fun and Recreation

In talking to new husbands about their relationship with their wives, another dominant theme emerges. New husbands and their wives share fun and enjoyment. Mutual activities seem to be carried out, not so much to appease one another but to jointly participate in something worthwhile. By way of contrast, an old husband I know commented upon his forthcoming trip to Toronto with his wife: "This should keep her happy for a while. Mary's favorite restaurant has $18 entrees. I think it's ridiculous, but it will keep her from pestering me for a week if I take her there. She can shop for most of the weekend and I'll drag along with her. The next time I want some time to myself on a weekend Mary won't think of five different things for me to do around the house." In essence, this old husband and his wife take turns having fun. The Toronto weekend will be Mary's turn. Her husband Ernie will get his turn for a few hours of fun at some unspecified future date.

Bruce, a new husband, is able to share fun and excitement with his wife: "Lenore and I have a blast together. The activities that come to mind are dancing, dining, hiking, playing tennis, conversation, and good varied sex together. So far, neither of us has any interest in swinging or asking a third party to join us in bed. When we do things together we both get a kick out of it. That doesn't mean that I enjoy everything Lenore does, or does she enjoy everything I do. We simply do those things alone so as not to get in each other's hair. To give you one example, my wife is a bug for antiquing. She forages for antiques with a couple of her close friends. If I went with her, it would be a drag for me and she would sense my attitude seeping through. My passion is stock car racing and demolition derbies. When one of these events comes to town that I want to see, I give Lenore advance notice and just go. Sometimes I go with a friend and sometimes I go by myself. I have no intention of dragging someone to the drag races who really doesn't want to go. Why throw bad experiences into a relationship that's working out so well?"

Sharing the Future

In a seminar I conduct in management and career development students are encouraged to participate in an exercise many have come to regard as intriguing and awakening. As part of an activity designed to foster self-awareness, students prepare a self-development dossier that many show to their spouses. Dean, a big company accountant, explains one unexpected result from his wife reading the dossier: "What an eye-opener to me and my wife. For the first time Ingrid was aware of what I was trying to accomplish in life. I guess I just had never told Ingrid that I someday wanted to run a small business of my own and move to a more rural area. She was under the impression that an accountant like myself would prefer to remain in a large city working for a major corporation. Now she could understand why I thought saving money was so important. It requires a good deal of capital to buy an ongoing business or start one from scratch.

"A discussion of my future led quite naturally to a discussion of her future. I learned that although Ingrid is not smoldering with discontent right now about being a full-time homemaker, she very much wants to change her life style in the direction of becoming a career woman. As we got heavier into the conversation, it became apparent that maybe our hopes for the future were congruent. Ingrid and I have always cooperated well on any joint venture we've undertaken such as decorating the home or planning the wedding. Maybe it would not be beyond reason for the two of us to open up a business together. An income tax preparation service in a semirural area, a pet store, or maybe a motel and restaurant. The possibilities are endless when the two of you are tuned in on the same wavelength."

Sharing the future in terms of sharing dreams and expectations is not a phenomenon peculiar to the new husband. For decades, young couples have looked at each other wistfully while talking about the long-range prospects of home ownership or raising a family. What is new in sharing the future is that new husbands and liberated husbands alike are planning for the future in terms of the quality of their relationship. Instead of dreaming only about acquiring material objects and children more couples are now trying to figure out where their relationship is headed. And not only couples in their early twenties.

At a couples' group, members were asked to share with each other the most important problem they were facing that they felt comfortable talking about. Thirty-seven-year-old Yves said, "Here is mine, and I know Josie (his live-in girlfriend) will back me up on this. Neither of us want to fall into the same old routine dullness trap that has plagued most of our married friends. We are actually making plans to avoid the live-together blahs. And it's working. We try to reach new levels of intimacy with others both emotionally and physically. The other day I told Josie a certain part of her anatomy was adorable even though she feels it is unattractive. (Josie feigns a grimace at that point.)

"One night, shortly after a long conversation on the topic of keeping our relationship alive, Josie pulled one of the cutest surprises since we started living together. I was lying in bed reading the *New York Review of Books,* when Josie walked into the room wearing a cowgirl hat, a lasso, knee length boots, and nothing else. I think I tore a stomach muscle laughing. Josie went through that routine as a demonstration that she was not going to let the blahs take over our relationship.

"Josie revealed to me recently that one of her biggest personal concerns about the future was what she could possibly do to become less obscure on this earth. We toyed around with all the possibilities. Josie decided that if she were able to sell or even give away a few of her paintings, it would make her immortal in a small but constructive way. She's now being tutored in painting and hopes to give a few paintings to friends next Christmas. If her friends hang them, Josie will have her signature hanging in somebody else's house. A small start, but certainly in the right direction.

"Sharing our past brought Josie and I pretty close together. Sharing the present also helps improve our relationship. But sharing our future has done the most for infusing a new level of intimacy into our relationship."

chapter 4

Dialogues and Monologues

"What's so good about my relationship with Alan?" replied Ramona. "I think I can pinpoint it with no trouble at all. Alan actually listens to me in a very positive way. Other men I have dated, even my former husband, rarely ever listened to me in a way that convinced me they cared what I was saying. When I have something I consider important to tell Alan, he focuses on what I am saying as if he were the one who initiated the topic. I know that everything I bring home to talk about isn't earth-shattering news, but Alan becomes totally absorbed in my thoughts. Perhaps Alan listens so well because he finds me interesting or because he loves me. Another possibility is that Alan likes women. Maybe for all three reasons. Whatever the reason behind his attentiveness, it makes for a grand relationship."

Ramona's ecstatic comments about her husband, Alan, underscore a distinguishing characteristic of new husbands—they tend to engage in dialogues rather than monologues with their wives and children. New husbands listen actively rather than passively. When a new husband and his wife are engaged in conversation, the pattern of interaction stands in clear contrast to an interaction between an old husband and wife. New husbands and their spouses *react* to each other's thoughts and feelings, while old husbands and their wives *take turns* talking.

Engaging in monologues rather than dialogues is often the difference between a vapid and a vibrant relationship. So important is this distinction that I have constructed a series of interchanges between husbands and wives or husbands and children to illustrate the difference between dialogues and monologues. Each conversation will be illustrated by first involving an old husband and then a new husband. Liberated husbands, as I define them, are also more prone to participate in dialogues rather than monologues. A note of caution. On occasion an old husband will engage in a dialogue and a new husband will engage in a monologue. This categorization of new husbands as opposed to old husbands and the corresponding description of their behavior in a variety of situations points to general tendencies, not absolute distinctions.

A Wife's Quest for Recognition

A. WIFE AND OLD HUSBAND

"An incredibly nice thing happened to me today. I learned that my painting, the one I've been working on for five months, will be hung at the Clothes Line Art Show this summer."

"By the way when you were down in the basement working on your painting, did you use my rubber insulated screwdriver? It's missing."

"Right now I don't give a damn about your screwdriver. Go look for it where you left it."

"What kind of an answer is that? If I knew where my screwdriver was, I wouldn't ask you."

B. WIFE AND NEW HUSBAND

"An incredibly nice thing happened to me. . . ."

"Terrific. I'm proud of you. You put a lot of energy into that project and now somebody is recognizing your talent. You must feel great."

"That's exactly how I feel—great. I couldn't be more pleased if I had won money in the state lottery. This gives me the courage to submit some more paintings for hanging."

"It's nice to have a talented wife. But remember, I discovered your talent first."

There's Something Wrong with Our Sex Life

A. WIFE AND OLD HUSBAND

"Dan, there is something I think we should talk about. Maybe you haven't noticed it, but our sex is becoming more and more routine. I haven't reached a climax in weeks. Five days ago was the last time we had sex and then you fell asleep right on top of me."

"Maybe you're just imagining things. I don't have any complaints about our sex. I'll let you know if our sex ever becomes a problem."

"You mean to tell me that you haven't noticed a problem?"

"That's what I said. Now drop the topic and let me mix you a drink."

B. WIFE AND NEW HUSBAND

"Dan, there is something I think we should talk about. Maybe you haven't noticed it, but. . . ."

"It sounds as if you've been disappointed with our sex together lately. Perhaps we do have a problem, perhaps we don't. I have noticed a difference in the quality of our sex, but I don't think it's been anything drastic. What do you see as the problem?"

"You don't seem to be really involved. If we had just met you would never fall asleep on top of me."

"Now I think we're getting at something important. I have not been as involved in our sex as in the past, mostly because I felt you have not been responsive to me. Both of us are sending out negative vibrations to each other. We're acting distant because we feel the other person is acting distant."

"I'm glad you're not angry that I brought the problem up. Maybe we can trace back to the circumstances surrounding the time our sex went from torrid to lukewarm. . . ."

Is It Our Money or Your Money?

A. WIFE AND OLD HUSBAND

"Bill, I thought of something when I signed the joint income tax form the other day. Although all our assets are shared by state law, our three banking accounts are in your name. Why is that? Don't you trust my judgment about financial matters?"

"Why are you complaining about a technical detail like that. It's the husband's job to protect his wife from having to worry about things like bank accounts. What's for dinner?"

"The whole thing doesn't sound quite right to me. I feel left out of things."

"You find the pickiest things to complain about."

B. WIFE AND NEW HUSBAND

"Bill, I thought of something when I signed the joint income tax form the other day. Although our assets are shared by state law. . . ."

"It sounds like you're discontented about the way I have arranged things financially. Maybe you feel you should have more power in these matters."

"Exactly. Your having total control over the bank accounts makes me feel like a second-class citizen in our marriage."

"My intent was not to make you feel like a second-class citizen. It's just been a long-held belief of mine that only one person in a marriage should be in charge of the bank accounts. How would having separate accounts appeal to you?"

"Maybe that would be a good compromise. I appreciate your not being pigheaded about the whole topic."

Hey Dad, I'm a Cheerleader Now!

A. SON AND OLD HUSBAND TYPE OF FATHER

"Dad, I've got the most terrific news. Thirty-five fellows tried out for the cheerleading squad and only five were chosen. I was one of them."

"What? Are you serious? I never thought I'd see the day when my son became a cheerleader. If you can jump like that, why not try out for the gymnastic team."

"Sorry I bothered you, Dad. Go on back to reading your newspaper."

"No bother, but I thought you said you had some terrific news."

B. SON AND NEW HUSBAND TYPE OF FATHER

"Dad, I've got the most terrific news. Thirty-five fellows tried out. . . ."

"Hey, that is terrific news. If cheerleading is your thing, go to it. I don't know too much about cheerleading, but I know it takes quite a bit of acrobatic skill."

"Dad, you are tough. I know that cheerleading isn't your sport, but I can tell you're happy that I'm happy. By the way, could you make it to any of the games?"

"How about the first game?"

I Need Some Time to Myself

A. WIFE AND OLD HUSBAND

"Larry, I feel the need for a change of routine. Next

weekend I'd like to take a trip to Philadelphia to visit Barbara, my roommate from my single days. Maybe the children could stay with you."

"Nice try. Just because you want to run off to Philadelphia and pretend you are single for a weekend, don't try to dump the kids on me. I'm not going to do your baby-sitting while you're away having fun. Take the kids with you, and then I can have some fun too."

"You're missing the whole point. I didn't say I wanted to be single for a weekend; I said I wanted a change of pace. Everybody needs to get away once in a while."

"Don't try and pull any of your cute tricks on me. What the hell is a married woman with children doing trying to run away for a weekend?"

"Okay, it's your loss, not the children's. I'm going to Philadelphia and the children can stay with my mother. At least they are welcome there."

"You are out of your mind."

B. WIFE AND NEW HUSBAND

"Larry, I feel the need for a change of routine. Next weekend. . . ."

"I can understand why you would like a change of routine. The kids and I will have a ball. Both children and I like fishing and you don't. While you're getting rejuvenated in Philly, the three of us can have a fun weekend of fishing and camping. Send us a postcard."

"I know I'll miss you three even though I'll have a good time."

Better Cut Down on the Chinese Food

A. WIFE AND OLD HUSBAND

"I've been feeling terrible lately. I seem to get more headaches than I have in the past. I've been dizzy at work and now my old back injury is acting up again."

"Aha, I know exactly what your problem is. I read a

newspaper article the other day about a woman with an identical problem. It seems that she began to eat too much Chinese food, just like we've been doing lately. Somehow the monosodium glutamate in the food got to her. As a result, she had all sorts of headaches, dizziness, and a bunch of other complaints."

"Thanks for the diagnosis, but maybe if you would listen to my complete story you might have a different opinion."

"Then don't listen to me. See what the doctor has to say."

B. WIFE AND NEW HUSBAND

"I've been feeling terrible lately. I seem to get more headaches than I have in the past. I've been dizzy. . . ."

"It sounds as if you've got something heavy that's bothering you whether it's physical or emotional. Tell me about it."

"Jeff, you're right. I haven't told my doctor or anybody else yet, but I'm beginning to think that maybe my body isn't working as well as it used to. Perhaps I'm afraid that the change of life is beginning to take hold. Maybe it's tough for me to admit that I look my age."

"Let me shut off the TV so I can concentrate on what you're talking about. It sounds heavy."

"Thanks for listening. I'm really worried, Jeff. . . ."

Many Men Are Fashion Conscious

A. WIFE AND OLD HUSBAND

"Burt, I've been noticing that you haven't bought any new clothing in a long time. Let's go shopping together and I'll help you select something that looks good on you. I know that men dislike shopping."

"Okay, so I do need some new clothing. I'll take you shopping with me so long as you promise not to take up the whole afternoon."

"I'm glad you agree. I want you to look nice, not like your wife doesn't care what you put on your back."

"I have to admit, picking out clothing is your department."

B. WIFE AND NEW HUSBAND

"Doug, I've been noticing that you haven't bought any new clothing in a long time. Let's go shopping together. . . ."

"What I really hear you saying is, because I'm a male, that automatically makes me insensitive to fashion and style. Your suggestion about buying new clothing is a good one. The reason I've been holding back is that I'm saving for some new ski equipment. But when I go shopping, I'll go alone."

"That certainly isn't the way most men think. Most men I know hate to shop for clothes. Besides, many more men than women are color-blind."

"True, many men dislike clothes shopping but I'm an individual. I'm capable of and willing to select my own clothing, just as you are capable of and willing to pick out your clothing. It's true that some men are clods in the fashion area but men are also the most significant force in the field of clothing design."

I Want to Be More Than a Plastic Surgeon's Wife

A. WIFE AND OLD HUSBAND

"Duane, tonight's party left me with that same disquieting feeling that's been plaguing me for the last couple of years. I've about had it with people referring to me as the wife of that successful plastic surgeon."

"You really are something. Complaining about being married to a plastic surgeon. Last year I made over $100,000. I didn't hear you complaining about being married to that kind of money."

"You're missing the point. I'm not complaining that

you don't make enough money. You're tops in that department. I'm not even complaining about you. I'm just sick and tired of being Mrs. Plastic Surgeon."

"Well if you'd rather be Mrs. Cab Driver or Mrs. Nobody, maybe that can be arranged. There are about one million women in this city who'd like to take your place."

"Just because my parents are Old World people, it doesn't mean that all my fulfillment in life can come from being married to a doctor, even if he makes a lot of money."

"For the life of me, I just cannot figure out what you're bitching about now."

B. WIFE AND NEW HUSBAND

"Ralph, tonight's party left me with that same disquieting feeling that's been plaguing me for the last couple of years. . . ."

"Okay, let's get this out on the table. There is something about being married to me that is bugging you."

"Maybe it isn't being married to you individually that's bugging me. It's the fact that so many people refer to me only in relation to you. It's as if my only identity stemmed from the person I married. Suppose our roles were reversed and people referred to you as 'that brunette fellow who married the most successful woman advertising executive in the city.'"

"I don't think I'd like it, but let's get back to your situation. How do you feel about achieving part of your identity from your marriage to me?"

"In a way I feel proud, and I wish you continued success in your work. But I also feel some resentment and anger. It's that anger that seems to be giving me headaches."

"What do you think you're really angry about?"

"I'm sure that it's anger about not being more of a person in my own right. Or maybe it's jealousy about your success. I want you to be successful but I want to be successful myself."

"I take it being a terrific homemaker and hostess don't make you feel successful enough?"

"Absolutely right. For me in today's world, that's not enough success."

"Okay, Cheryl, now that you've defined the problem, what do you intend to do about it?"

"I'm not sure yet exactly what it is that I'll do. One think I know for sure though is that I'll do something that will make me feel more significant as an individual. I've been having fantasies about someday owning a small art store specializing in natural art such as driftwood and curious looking rocks."

"Fortunately we're in a financial position to shake loose some venture capital."

"Let's break out some wine to celebrate a conversation that could be a turning point in my life."

Let's Try Something Different Tonight

A. GIRLFRIEND AND OLD HUSBAND TYPE OF BOYFRIEND

"Chet, let's try something different tonight. I've been reading about some wild, new bedtime tricks. All we need is four small sections of rope, and a little imagination."

"What in the world are you talking about?"

"I'm talking about trying something new sexually. It's not that complicated. We begin by you lying face up on the bed without any clothing. I then tie a rope to both of your arms and legs. Then I tie your arms and your ankles to the four legs of the bed. Next I'll stimulate you with my mouth until the pleasure is almost too much for you. Now wait until you hear the rest before you make any suggestions or criticisms. After your turn it's my turn. You bind me up and then stimulate me orally until I'm tingling with excitement. Then, it's your turn to be tied down, but this time I sit on top of you and we have intercourse from that position. How about it?"

"What the hell has come over you? You're becoming a pervert. It's absolutely sick. If the cops ever broke in while one of us were tied up we'd wind up in jail."

"You're calling me a pervert simply because you're afraid to try anything exciting. That's the trouble with our relationship, you're too conservative."

"You're weird and you're sick. I thought I was living with a decent American girl. Any more of these perverted ideas and I'm leaving."

"Big threat. I own most of the stuff in our apartment anyway. I didn't know I was living with a Puritan."

B. GIRLFRIEND AND NEW HUSBAND TYPE OF BOYFRIEND

"Cal, let's try something different tonight. I've been reading about some wild, new bedtime tricks. All we need is. . . ."

"Sounds pretty good so far, tell me more."

"I'm talking about trying something new sexually. It's not that complicated. We begin by you lying face up. . . ."

"You are terrific. I'm getting excited already."

"Then you like my idea?"

"Honey, it's almost a perfect idea."

"I take it you have some reservations about my idea?"

"No problem with your idea. I just want to make things a little bit more interesting. I'll get us a nice, small tree branch. While I'm tied up, you beat me gently with the branch. I'll do the same while you're tied up. From what I've heard, the whole experience is very sensuous."

"Fine with me. I don't mind branching out a bit in our sex life."

Whoever Saw a Want Ad for an Anthropologist?

A. DAUGHTER AND OLD HUSBAND TYPE OF FATHER

"Oh, by the way, Dad, I've finally decided upon what I'm going to study in college this fall."

"It's about time. I've invested about $6,000 so far in your college education. It's about time you've reached a decision that could make that kind of investment worthwhile."

"I'm not sure what you mean by worthwhile, but I have hit upon something that's important to me."

"I'm eager to hear your news."

"I've decided to major in anthropology. I've met some absolutely stimulating professors and students in that field."

"Anthropology? You said anthropology. That's absurd. Nobody majors in anthropology. I can't name you one person who has majored in that field."

"What's so absurd about majoring in anthropology?"

"I'll give you a good reason. Nobody works as an anthropologist. I've never even seen a want ad for an anthropologist."

"Your comment is irrelevant. I'm majoring in anthropology so I can develop a better understanding how people are shaped by the world around them. Maybe that way I can even come to understand myself a little better."

"You're in for a surprise when you face that cold world outside. Maybe you should enroll in a college of business."

B. SIMILAR SITUATION BETWEEN DAUGHTER AND NEW HUSBAND TYPE OF FATHER

"Oh, by the way, Dad, I've finally decided upon what I'm going to study in college this fall."

"Interesting, tell me about it."

"I've decided to major in anthropology. I've met some absolutely stimulating professors and students in that field."

"I'm happy for you. I'm glad you've reached a decision. Could you tell me a little about what anthropology deals with?"

"It's complicated and, from what I hear, anthropologists can't even give you a good definition of anthropology. I think anthropology is really the study of mankind. It helps us understand how we've come to be what we are."

"Sounds heavy to me. Maybe, if I had to do it all over again, I might want to study something exotic like that."

"You mean then, Father, that you actually approve of my studying anthropology?"

"Why not, anything that can help us understand people better might help unscrew this screwed-up world. What do you intend to do with your knowledge about anthropology?"

"If I prove to be a top student, I'll probably go on to graduate study. Besides that I hope to use anthropology as a better way of understanding myself."

"I don't want to be obtuse, but what does a person do with a graduate degree in anthropology?"

"There's lots of research going on these days that requires the skills of an anthropologist. Besides, most colleges and universities offer courses in anthropology that need somebody to teach them."

"The idea is growing on me already. Up until this moment, I never thought about having an anthropologist in the family."

Why This Difference Between Old and New Husbands?

Assuming these observations are correct that new husbands tend to engage in dialogues with their spouses and children, while old husbands engage in monologues—

or at least are poor listeners—it is worthwhile to explore the reasons for this difference. Understanding the reasons for these differences could represent the first step toward breaking down the communication barriers that are so frequently erected between old husbands and members of their families.

One curious observation about many old husbands is that they actually dislike women, or at least feel somewhat uncomfortable in their presence. One clue to this dislike or discomfort is that many old husbands prefer males to females as playmates. They would rather spend free time with males than with females, particularly their wives. Many old husbands rarely bring any problem of significance to attention of their wives. New husbands, in contrast, basically like and feel comfortable with women.

Although new husbands do not avoid male companionship, they actually enjoy the companionship of their wives. In the latter regard, the new husband must be differentiated from the *pseudo* new husband. Husbands of this kind dislike spending significant amounts of time with their wives but do so in order to maintain harmony at home. What their wives have to say is of little or no interest to them, but they suffer through these hours of gnawing discontentment in order to have some pleasure at meal time and bedtime. As one old husband explained, "I get along just fine with my wife. She's good in the kitchen, good in bed, and she makes a good mother. What more does a man need?"

Old husbands and their wives often engage in monologues rather than dialogues because they have lost an essential ingredient to meaningful communication between two people—a joint purpose in life. As the years advance, old husbands and their wives gradually drift apart psychologically until they are leading separate lives. Verbal communication between the two becomes as perfunctory as their sex lives together. New husbands and their wives do not inevitably have ideal relationships, but they rarely let a relationship deteriorate to the point where dialogue is impossible.

A new husband is, by definition, a person who is attuned to the nuances of male-female relationships. When a new husband and his wife are beginning to drift apart, both partners are likely to recognize the situation. When a realignment of a shared purpose in life becomes impossible, the new husband and his wife are willing to reevaluate their marriage. For the new husband and his wife, the anguish of separation and divorce is less painful than the anguish of communication between the two being only ceremonial.

Another factor that deters meaningful dialogue between old husbands and their wives is that the majority of old husbands take a sexist viewpoint of marital relationships. As sexists, they see clearly defined differences in the male and female roles. Holding a rigid distinction between the activities of a male versus female in a marital relationship, they find it difficult to communicate effectively with the "other camp." Similarly, some engineers find it difficult to communicate with salesmen and some psychiatrists find it difficult to communicate with social workers. One old husband noted, "My wife takes her problems to her mother or girlfriend. I admit she's better off. It's always been hard for me to understand women."

Another reason old husbands prefer monologues (or even very limited conversations) to dialogues is that they fear an equal relationship with their wives. To engage in meaningful dialogue with another person requires breaking down the notion that one individual is superior to another. When two people freely exchange ideas they must, at minimum, show equal respect for each other's ideas. One-way communication is the usual mode when two individuals have unequal power in the relationship—such as a prison guard and a prisoner.

Consciously or unconsciously equating an egalitarian relationship with a loss of power and control in the marriage and family, the old husband prefers one-way to two-way communication. During a workshop designed to help homemakers figure out a path to obtaining employment outside the home, one group member vociferously complained about her discontent as a homemaker. Asked by another woman if she had ever voiced these discontents to her husband, the first woman replied: "Oh, I have many times but it doesn't do any good. My husband doesn't listen to me. He thinks that, if I get a job, I'll have more say around the house."

chapter 5

The Restoration of Fatherhood

Fatherhood has become an exciting, alive experience for those men who take a new husband approach to child rearing. Gradually, an increasing number of men—included in their ranks are married males, live-in boyfriends, divorced men, and a handful of bachelors—are discovering that an active involvement in child rearing adds a vital dimension to life. New husbands are not merely assisting their wives or girlfriends with child rearing, they are playing a major, independent role in the children's development. Don, a welder and new husband type of father, represents this parental philosophy in his statement:

"Don't lay that 'I see you help your wife with the children' bit on me. If anything, Darlene helps *me* out. Working the second shift frees up loads of time that I can spend with my son and daughter. When one of the kids gets a fever, it could be me as well as my wife who pops a thermometer into his mouth."

Before delving further into the way in which new husbands relate to their progeny, it is imperative to examine some of the damage wrought—often quite unintentionally—by old husbands and, in some cases, totally liberated husbands. No one style of being a parent works best for all children, but approaches to fathering other than that of the new husband have created some serious problems for the children and society.

The Downgraded Father Image

The new husband style of fatherhood may salvage the image of fatherhood in North America, but considerable damage has already been wrought at various social levels in society. Fathers to the children of women receiving public assistance are notoriously weak as father images. Black and white "welfare boyfriends" are generally ineffectual as fathers and providers. A typical arrangement in these families is for the woman to secure an apartment contending to the social agency that the child's or children's father has abandoned them. Once moved in, the woman is joined by the boyfriend or husband. His contribution to family expenses is usually quite small.

It could rightfully be argued that as culturally disadvantaged males attain better educational and job opportunities they will become less discouraged. This lessened discouragement with life could readily result in more active participation in family activities.

A landlord of several buildings occupied by welfare tenants describes a sampling of the inadequate behavior of the so-called welfare boyfriend. "I just don't know how those women put up with those lazy guys. Whenever I come to collect the rent, night or day, you can find a boyfriend or husband sleeping. I've just about given up trying to get a male living there to help fix up the property. If I buy them paint and brushes, the man usually waits for the woman to do the painting. If he decides to do it himself, you can count on a wall half-done.

"After a fight the man usually leaves for a few days and the woman contends that he'll never be back. As soon as he runs out of money he usually returns home. I guess that's only natural if the guy is unemployable. What I can't accept is the boyfriend's reluctance to help his woman out with even the most minor chore. One of my tenants, Geraldine, was having a baby. She called me from the hospital to explain that her rent check would be late because she left it behind when she entered the hospital. I asked Geraldine if her boyfriend could mail the check. She told me that she had asked him to do that for her, but since it was already signed he spent it on other things."

The image of fathers from higher social classes has not gone unscathed. Lawrence H. Fuchs, in *Family Matters,* reports the results of an informal but significant study conducted in an upper-middle-class suburban school near Boston. A teacher asked ten- and eleven-year-old children, "What does it mean to be a father?" Fuchs writes:

> Not one of the thirteen boys and only six of the twenty-three girls had even one good thing to say about being a father. The principal theme was that fathers were tense and harried, overwhelmed by responsibility and work. One boy wrote, "You have to pay the rent, keep the family healthy, make sure that the lawn is mowed, the yard is neat." Another said, "I wouldn't want to be a father because you would have to go to work all day and spank the kids and listen to their crying and would have to listen to them talk back and you would have to learn how to make love and that's hard. . . ."[1]

Fuchs writes further about the girls questioned, who held a similar critical view of the father image:

> Typical was the girl who said that being a father means ". . . making good money and getting a good job. Feeding your family. Paying the bills. Coming home to hear the problems. Going to work every morning. Coming home with a headache."[2] Some girls volunteered that being a father was more difficult than being a mother.

Bruno Bettelheim, the well-publicized University of Chicago child psychologist, has equally critical commentary about society's perception of the father. He contends that the father image has been downgraded both in the eyes of mothers and other significant people. One of the underlying problems, according to Dr. Bettelheim, is that most middle-class fathers no longer receive the adulation of their sons. As he observes in an article written for *Playboy:*

> For ages, the father, as a farmer, as a craftsman working in the shop, had been very visible to his sons and, because of his physical prowess and know-how in doing real things in the real world, was an object of envious adulation. Now, the mother who traditionally is the one who nurtures the child becomes ever more the carrier of authority. If for no other reason than that she is with the child during the father's waking hours, the mother becomes the disciplinarian, the value giver, who tells the child all day long what goes and what does not. In short, mother knows best, and father next to nothing.[3]

The American father's preoccupation with watching sports on television has also contributed substantially to a downgrading of his image. Undeniably, a high proportion of fathers who regularly watch sporting events on television do so out of frustration and boredom with their lives. Watching superior athletes perform is a normal human pastime. However, the fan obsessed with sports who avoids active involvement with his family in order to watch other males perform is not unlike the husband who prefers masturbation to sexual intercourse with his wife. While masturbating he can fantasize relations with any woman he chooses. Intercourse with his wife is much more routine.

Although mention of the television-watching male sports enthusiast is often humorous, the humor is not flattering. Children in the presence of peers rarely brag about their father's prowess at watching television, but they do brag about a father's even mediocre competence in a participative sport. During a little league practice session, one ten-year-old bragged to another about his own father's capacity to hit long fly balls. Nonplused at first, his friend replied, "Yeah, but my Dad's real good at hitting grounders."

The Absentee Father

A popular show business figure rushed home from an out-of-town engagement to be with his son who had just been admitted to a city hospital, suffering acute symptoms of drug overdose. Emergency measures saved the son's life. The young man's first words to his father were, "Who the hell are you? Who needs you now?"

A chemist received a letter from his oldest child from whom he had not heard in over a year. In great detail the son explained how living with a male lover had become a peak life experience. The chemist bemoaned to his wife,

"What in God's name did I ever do wrong? I knew there was something wrong with our son. He would never talk to me about anything. Why didn't he just tell me he wasn't a normal male? I would have sought help for him."

Both of these fathers are experiencing some of the possible consequences of being an absentee father. In the case of the entertainer, physical absence as a father could have contributed to the son's emotional conflicts, which were severe enough to lead to drug abuse. In contrast, the chemist was physically present but psychologically absent. His noninvolvement in his child's world contributed to the development of his son's gayness. Many people would rightfully argue that homosexual preference is no less desirable than a heterosexual preference. However, if the father is chagrined because his son is gay *and* the son finds his own gayness a source of deep personal conflict, then the son's homosexual preference constitutes a problem.

Paternal absenteeism does not inevitably lead to adverse consequences in the development of a child, but the pattern is pronounced enough to conclude that having an involved, caring father who is physically and mentally available does make a difference. Does this mean that most children who lack live-in fathers are doomed to a chaotic personal adjustment later in life? Decidedly not, for two major reasons. First, many children without live-in fathers have active relationships with their fathers outside the home and spend time with them on a predictable and regular basis. A new husband type of father whether he lives in the home, is separated, or divorced characteristically responds quite well to the psychological needs of his child or children.

The situation of a nonexistent (deceased or departed) father is more complex. Here a boy or girl often is fortunate enough to find a father surrogate such as a boyfriend of the mother, uncle, older brother, or even a friend. A few children of absentee fathers are thus able to find a suitable replacement who functions reasonably well as a father. Now for a consideration of some of the problems absentee fathers often *do* create for their progeny.

According to research evidence gathered by Henry B. Biller for his book, *Father, Child, and Sex Role,* an absentee father may have adverse effects upon a son's self-image as a male. The impact is likely to be more far-reaching when the father is absent during the first several years of life. Many liberated males and females would argue that a strong male self-image is not necessarily desirable, but traditional psychologists, however, feel such a self-image contributes positively to a man's interpersonal relationships. Conversely, a weak male self-image can lead a boy to behave in ways that create strained and impoverished interpersonal relationships. Here are a few examples of the kinds of inappropriate behavior shown by some young males with weak masculine self-images.

Tim, age fourteen, carries out a virtual vendetta against girls. When asked by his father why he doesn't want to attend his junior high school dance, Tim replies, "I hate girls. Only a girl would want to dance with a girl."

Paul, age nine, has a rigid classification of toys and sports as being male or female. He refuses to play tennis with his sister because "That's not a sport for boys." When receiving a gift from a relative such as a green ball-point pen, he inquires "Are you sure green is a boy's color?"

Mario, age fifteen, contends that he will never marry because of the pressures placed upon married men in this country. Claims Mario, "Only a fool would want a wife. Who wants to get stuck with worrying about a wife and children? The man has to pay for everything."

Absentee fathers frequently have sons who exhibit

many of the characteristics and mannerisms contemporary cultural standards define as feminine—an elusive and changeable notion. Apparently, some sons who lack physically present fathers slowly begin to model their mothers' (or sometimes sisters') traits and mannerisms. Frequently—but not inevitably—effeminate males are emotionally closer to their mothers than their fathers. One might speculate that the dramatic increase in the number of effeminate young men is attributable in large measure to a generation of fathers whose work responsibilities interfered with their spending suitable amounts of time with their sons. An equally plausible explanation is that the increased acceptance of effeminate behavior among males in our society has encouraged more males to behave in effeminate ways. Young males are simply less concerned about conforming to a male stereotype.

Underlying character traits are of greater significance than superficial characteristics of masculine or feminine behavior. Male children of absentee fathers are much more likely to be passive, dependent, and timid than their counterparts with physically present fathers. Exceptions abound, but an assertive, independent, and outgoing father who spends considerable time with his children will probably inculcate similar behavior traits in them. (Mothers, too, can influence their children in such directions, but in this book we are concerned more about fathers than mothers.)

Dr. Biller notes that an adequate father contributes to his son's masculine *sex-role adoption*. He notes, "In terms of masculinity, the degree of the individual's assertiveness, competitiveness, independence, and activity directed toward physical prowess and mastery of his environment should be taken into account. An unmasculine adoption seems represented by behaviors such as passivity, dependency, and timidity."[4]

The distinction between superficial behavior and underlying character traits is particularly evident in the situation of an effeminate but highly accomplished male. A well-known merchandiser in New York is effeminate in external behavior almost to the point of burlesque, yet he is a competitive and aggressive business person with a high degree of independence. Among the many possible early life influences on this man could have been the combination of an accomplished mother and a weak father model. Another combination producing the same result could have been a satisfactory mother figure and an effeminate but accomplished father.

Absence of the father can also have a profound impact upon the psychological well-being of the daughter. Among the research findings culled by Biller is the notion that the girl with an absent father "may lack certain experiences which make it difficult for her to interact with males." In order for a girl to develop a healthy self-picture of a feminine person, she needs encouragement of her femininity by a father or father figure. In one study, women who claimed to lack an available father in childhood had less feminine self-concepts than women who spent more time with their fathers during childhood.

A woman's sexual adjustment can also be adversely affected by the unavailability of a father in early life. One study indicated that women with absent fathers manifested frequent complaints of not being able to achieve satisfactory sexual relationships with their husbands. Beginning life with a negative relationship with a father often carries over into negative relationships with males in general later in life. One woman in her mid-twenties gives her evaluation of why she has so many problems in forming good relationships with men:

"Jeb, my father, was really nothing to me. Half the time he wasn't around. When he was around, he was usually drunk. When I date a man I expect too much of him. He has to be both a boyfriend and a father to me. Then when he tries to father me, I only rebel against him. Since it's very hard for one person to be both a father and a boyfriend, most of my relationships just don't meet my expectations."

The devaluation of maleness and masculinity so common in homes deprived of paternal presence or involvement often adversely affects girls. Many investigators, according to Biller, have observed that black girls in families where the father is absent or ineffectual develop hostile and derogatory attitudes toward males. A black female, working as a supervisor in a nursing home, commented about her perceptions of males: "My mother taught me to believe that all males are pricks. For a while I thought Mamma was wrong. Now with two little children at home and no child support from their father, I've come to agree with her. Men are just basically irresponsible."

The Unisexual Child

George, a totally liberated husband, and his hotly feminist wife, Tilda, share a common philosophy of child rearing. Leslie and Terry (their son and daughter, respectively) are raised under the same atmosphere of sex-role blurring. George expounds upon their notions about raising "free" children:

"Tilda and I both very much want Leslie and Terry to be nonsexists. We are both working hard to overcome the sexist thinking imposed upon children by society. We've purged our library at home of those horrid children's books that define maleness in terms of accomplishment and aggressiveness; and femaleness in terms of passivity and noninvolvement in the outside world.

"We show our children by our very actions that there is no essential difference in the male and female role. We encourage our son Leslie to fondle kittens and girl dolls in order to help him develop tenderness and a desire for child rearing. Terry is told that she might want to be the provider in her family, assuming she decides to bear children as an adult.

"When the talk turns to choosing an adult occupation, as it often does over dinner, we talk about job levels for people, not male or female occupational roles. For instance, when we talk about the medical field we emphasize that nursing is a good job for somebody who enjoys taking care of other people. I found a photo of a male nurse in an Army medical journal and I pinned it on the bulletin board. We talk about being a doctor as a job for a person who wants to help people, but who also is into power and prestige. Terry showed some interest, so we bought her an authentic stethoscope.

"Dress is another area in which we want our children to be free. Leslie and Terry wear similar clothing. Neither my wife nor I are opposed to males and females wearing different styles of clothing, but we prefer that our own children escape sexist habits. Much of the time our children wear about the same style of clothing. We avoid with a passion any clothing that smacks of overdrawn male versus female stereotypes. A well-meaning uncle brought Leslie a pair of pajamas decorated with male sport figures, most of whom were shown prize fighting, playing hockey, football, baseball, and so forth. At the same time he gave Terry a pair of pajamas decorated with figures of girls doing the ballet, ice skating, and swimming. I accepted the gifts graciously, but then hid them away in a closet."

George and Tilda are only two people among a growing number of parents who contribute toward the development of unisex children—those who feel that male and female roles in society should overlap almost completely. In the past society has perhaps imposed overly rigid definitions of maleness and femaleness, but a unisex mode of life creates problems of its own. Dr. Benjamin Spock recently told a *Time* reporter he has qualms about sons and daughters being raised with minimal sexual distinction: "No country I know of has tried to bring them up to think of themselves as 'similar. Such an attempt would be the most unprecedented social experiment in the history of our species."

Kim, Harold, and Billie are three young adults who have come to reject culturally imposed sex roles. And in each of their lives there is an area of chronic dissatisfaction because of his or her discomfort with the male or female sex role. All three seem to have been raised in a home environment that encouraged a blurring of the distinctions between sexes.

Kim, age twenty-three, has recently entered psychotherapy because of her bitter dislike of the maternal role. She decided to go through with an unplanned pregnancy and now feels she made the wrong decision. In therapy she makes comments like these: "Blair and I had a good relationship until the baby came along. Now my resentment about being a mother is spilling over into our relationship. I'm picking on Blair when I should really be picking on myself for having been careless enough to become pregnant. I never wanted to get pregnant. I never wanted to be a mother. I hated caring for the baby from the start and the situation is getting worse every day."

Harold, age twenty-four, a graduate student in sociology, freely divulged some of his discontents in a rap session about male and female roles. "I just can't get into the male *machismo* thing. I've held a few part-time jobs here and there but I just couldn't imagine becoming a nine-to-five organization man. Maybe that's why I drifted toward the college professor racket. But now that I've been around a university for a while, it looks like the same rat race in that kind of life.

"I just can't see myself beating my brains out every day trying to increase the size of my 'academic penis' by publishing research studies about trivia. The pressure for publishing is greater for males than females despite the advances of the women's movement. If I do take a teaching job, it will be one where I can escape trying to conform to the big-strong-male-researcher mold.

"My other problem is really just another aspect of the male rat race. Right now I share half a house with two other fellows. Maybe I'm getting too old to live this way, but I don't want to live alone and I certainly don't want a woman dependent upon me. I just couldn't see putting myself in a situation where a person I lived with expected me to perform financially and sexually whenever it met her fancy. And then if I didn't come up with money for a new car, or a big stiff erection, she would put me down as a person. I'm looking for another way of life."

Billie, another product of an androgynous upbringing, is biologically male. His current life style is fashionably bisexual. Despite his avant-garde orientation, he is discontent about the neither/nor quality of his life. He laments: "Right now I don't know which way to turn. I'm not gay nor am I exclusively straight. As a young child my parents dressed me in girl's clothing which I seemed to like at the time. During the early years in school, I took the usual verbal assaults handed out in our society to delicate and sensitive males. Perhaps not a week would go by without some lout calling me 'queer,' 'faggot,' or 'sweetie.' As the times changed, so did the nouns and adjectives.

"Now antagonists call me 'Billie-Bi' which about describes my situation. Last time a few friends of mine and I were hanging out at the Bistro, we were trying to decide if we had a better chance of going home with a fellow or a girl. As things have worked out, I really can't enjoy sex with males or females. I get on some kind of guilt trip when I'm making it with a male. On the other hand, there's something basically revolting about putting your sex organ inside a wet vagina. Maybe I should try living with a fellow and a girl the way one of my friends does. Maybe after a year of that I could reach a decision about which direction to go. I think it would give me more peace of mind to be homosexual or heterosexual rather than bisexual."

Father as Child Rearer

A distinguishing characteristic of the new husband in his father role, as mentioned earlier, is his active involvement in child rearing. A new husband style of father looks upon raising his child or children as a serious life commitment that he and his wife (if on the scene) participate in jointly. Although in many home situations the woman still has an edge over the man in total number of hours spent in contact with children, a new husband style of father also logs in a considerable number of child-rearing hours.

Mothers of school-age children frequently spend no more time in direct contact with their children than do fathers—even when the mother happens to be a full-time homemaker. One suburban homemaker noted: "During the days I'm more like a hotel manager than a mother. The children don't see me until they come back for dinner late in the afternoon. After school they hop right out to see their friends. Now I'm trying to implement a mandatory system whereby the two children spend at least five minutes at home between school and their daily junket into the neighborhood."

Fathers with a new husband view of the world

participate in a full range of activities with their children from changing diapers to informal college and career counseling. Such fathers involve themselves in both routine activities with their children (such as prodding them about washing their hands or brushing their teeth and supervising household chores) and in the recreational realm. Raising children means much more to a new husband style of father than showing them off, disciplining them, and serving as a sports partner. The new husband type of father is the kind of man most likely to attend parent-teacher conferences and school plays.

All the new husbands participating in my research think that a father should play an active role in child rearing—quite often as active as or more active than the role played by the mother. Hank, a Mobile, Alabama, husband, father, and industrial foreman, provides an illuminating example of how new husbands feel about parenthood. In response to my question, "How active a role should a father play in child rearing?" Hank responded:

"Active. I feel that children will have a more balanced personality if both father and mother are active in rearing the children. If the father neglects his duties the children become mother-oriented, and often find it difficult to relate easily to men in society. I discovered this fact accidentally.

"Pregnancy upset my wife's hormone balance in some way so that her skin became hypersensitive to water. I had to handle all the chores involving wetting of the skin: washing dishes, scrubbing floors, cleaning the bathtub, basins, and sink, doing the laundry, bathing the baby, and even bathing my wife. Although I was working long hours at the time, my infant daughter and I spent 'happy hours' together while I was bathing her and getting her ready for bed. This period of time gave my wife a respite from tending the baby so that after the baby was put to bed, we did dishes together (with me washing and her drying).

"During those infant bath sessions, I taught my daughter crazy little rhymes, funny little songs ('The Three Little Fishes' and 'Mairzy Doats' were two of her favorites), how to count to ten in English, French, German, and Spanish, how to pronounce long words (for example, amphibious, ambidextrous), how to spell simple words—all of this before she was four years old. This relationship carried over into her school years—helping her with her school projects, and so on. Yet my daughter is almost a carbon copy of my wife in their mental and philosophical processes as well as physically."

Successful Career Men Can Be Active Fathers

"It's certainly no easy task," said Baxter, industrial engineering vice-president in a multiplant company. "My job can easily gobble up many more hours than the standard work week. If I just spent five days per year at each one of our plants, I'd be away from home over fifty nights during the year. When I can, I try to juggle trips around big events in my children's life such as birthdays, little league championship games, or water ballet shows. Last year I scheduled my visit to our European operations during the time in which my children were in summer camp. I try to make good use of time during the day so I don't have to drag home an attache case full of paper work every night.

"Although time with my children is precious, I'm not willing to sacrifice my executive career in order to be home every night at 5:30. Aside from spending loads of time with my children, I also want to serve as a person they can emulate—a guy who's making it in the big, tough outside world."

Baxter, like many of his new husband counterparts, is

both a successful career person and an involved, active father. In the following chapter, how a new husband juggles the demands of both his career and family is further examined. For now it suffices to glimpse at the opinion several successful new husbands have toward their personal involvement in child rearing.

Dr. Robert A. Braun, former technical manager and now practitioner of structural integration ("Rolfing"): "I'm in favor of an active role for a father. I have enjoyed playing with the kids at all ages. I related to the kids using little if any power that I could use to control them. All along I wanted to find ways to help the kids to be independent while providing the security they need to develop. Providing a reasonably good model of a mature male is one of a father's responsibilities."

John T. Shoup, a director of personnel development: "As a father I want to have an active role in child rearing. It is important for children to experience males as fathers and as they relate to females, and to experience fathers in traditional female roles."

Tom Aldrich, architect: "A father should play a very active role in raising children, especially in showing how a wife should be treated as a woman and a mother. This is usually copied by the children in later life. Disrespect for the mother should be dealt with firmly."

Dr. Andrew J. Snope, chairman of a biology department at a university: "A father should play a role equal to that of the mother. There is no evidence that one parent plays a more important role than the other. Besides two persons have more to offer than one; and each parent can do a better job when the burden in shared."

Edward V. Whirty, a manpower planner: "A father should play a strong, loving role. The typical disciplinary role should be abandoned. The father should supply an identification role exhibiting firm control yet extending love and concern."

The Masculine, Confident Son

If a father wants to raise a son to be masculine and self-confident, his best child-rearing approach would be that of a new husband. An analysis of a large number of research studies led Henry B. Biller to conclude, "A warm relationship with a father who is himself secure in his masculinity is a crucial factor in the boy's masculine development. Boys who have punitive, rejecting fathers or passive, ineffectual fathers generally have less adequate sex-role functioning than do boys who have interested-nurturant fathers who play a salient and decisive role in family interactions."[5] Additionally, a father who sets limits to his son's behavior is also crucial to that child's masculine development.

Four aspects of fatherhood thus seem crucial in assisting a male child in becoming masculine and confident: serving as a masculine model, setting the limits of tolerable behavior, playing a decisive role in the family situation, and maintaining a close affectionate relationship with the child. When a father overemphasizes one of these aspects at the expense of others, the son may not develop a masculine, confident pattern. For instance, the father who overemphasizes the power role in the family situation but neglects being affectionate toward his son may produce a child who retreats from masculine (and into feminine) behavior later in life. As aptly described in *Father, Child, and Sex Role:*

> The stereotype of the masculine hardworking father whose primary activity at home is lying on the couch, watching television, or sleeping is an all too accurate description of

> many fathers. If the boy's father is not consistently involved in family functioning, it is much harder for his son to learn to be appropriately assertive, active, aggressive, and independent.[6]

To combine the four essential requisites (masculinity, setting limits, making decisions, and giving affection) successfully is not easy for one father. A stockbroker commented about his relationship with his children: "In recent years I've been doing a lot of studying and rapping about what makes for a good male parent. The message I'm getting is that I should try to stay involved and interested in what my children are doing and feed them ample amounts of love. But, wow, when I drag home after one of those very bleak days on Wall Street, it's tough to respond to anything but a martini. On explosively good days, I do a much better job of parenting, but still it's hard to shake those stock quotations out of my head. I think I make the best parent when Wall Street has an average day."

The Feminine, Confident Daughter

Daughters as well as sons are profoundly influenced in a positive direction by the presence of a masculine, involved father (or father figure) throughout childhood. A consistent research finding is that women who feel good about their femaleness (whether they are career persons or full-time homemakers) were raised by fathers who encouraged their feminine behavior. Femininity, similar to many other subtle aspects about people's behavior, is essentially a subjective and cultural concept. It is far easier, however, to describe a given female as being feminine or nonfeminine than to abstractly define the notion. Feminine, in the context used here, refers to charm, grace, poise, and both physical and psychological attractiveness.

Fathers often play a more crucial role than mothers in encouraging the development of feminine characteristics in their daughters. This is true because fathers, more so than mothers, vary their approach to interacting with a particular child, depending upon whether that child is male or female. For instance, the same father might administer physical punishment to his son, but not to his daughter.

A new husband type of father provides an important contribution to his daughter's femininity via his relationship with the mother. A father who treats his wife with dignity and respect imprints the idea upon his daughter that females are worthy of respect and have dignity. In addition, to quote again from Henry Biller, ". . . if the father and mother mutually satisfy and value each other, the child (male or female) is much better able to learn effective interpersonal skill."[7]

Naomi, a feminine and ambitious accountant, points to the kinds of interactions many new husbands have with their daughters that help a woman become feminine and confident: "Dad is still my favorite male, but my current boyfriend is running a close second. Of course I was 'Daddy's little girl,' but our relationship went far beyond that. Dad was willing to listen while I rambled away about a variety of topics. He was truly interested in my opinions. When we did anything together, whether it was skiing or going to the bank, Dad treated me as if I were his date. He opened doors for me, made sure I was comfortable, and smiled at me frequently. No, I'm not looking for a husband or boyfriend to replace my father, but Dad did show me what it feels like to be treated like a woman."

Coping with the World

In summary, a new father helps his child better cope with the world. Undoubtedly, this is his biggest potential contribution to the long-range welfare of his children. Evidence is accumulating that an involved, affectionate, caring father with a secure masculine identification of his own helps a child develop the capabilities to cope more effectively in both the social and occupational realms. A sampling of some of this evidence follows.

A study conducted about a decade ago by M.G. Gruenbaum indicated that one group of underachieving schoolboys tended to have fathers who felt generally inadequate and considered themselves failures. In this situation, the fathers' negative self-pictures tended to serve as poor models for their sons. Compulsively achieving fathers who tried to impose their obsession with success upon the children might also drive their children toward underachievement. Somehow, fathers who behave as new husbands seem to find the appropriate balance in serving as models to their children.

A focused understanding of how an involved, caring father model influences the development of his children is obtained from evidence about the paternal styles of the fathers of juvenile delinquents (at least the fathers of those caught!). Delinquents and their fathers have notoriously poor long-standing relationships—even when the father lives at home. Several research studies have shown that the relationship between delinquent sons and fathers is marked by rejection, hostility, and antagonism. This finding appears to be true for delinquents from all class levels. Asked by a psychologist what his father was likely to say when he learned of his car theft, the young man replied: "I know exactly what he will say: 'I told you, you'll never amount to anything unless you shape up.'"

Many of the basic skills of relating to women are learned early in a boy's life as he observes his father relate to his mother (or in many cases to the father's new wife or girlfriend). Ideally, the boy learns that he can relate comfortably to women without feeling intimidated by them or experiencing the need to dominate them constantly. Although the father is not used as an exclusive model for learning how to deal with women, his influence is significant.

Finally, a new husband type of father provides his son with the basic tools to mold the future of society. Without these tools society will continue to plod along in the same destructive, sometimes effective, but more often ineffective, manner. As a consequence of having experienced positive fathering himself, the son is himself more able to become a successful father.

chapter 6

Career and Family Success

Ambitious, career-minded men entertain a variety of perspectives about how a wife and children fit into their quest for worldly success. And this perspective is inextricably related to the basic style of husband a man happens to be—old husband (including the organization man type), totally liberated husband, or new husband.

Old husbands typically have a noble, but inaccurate and incomplete, view of how career and family are related. An old husband often views his work as a vehicle for bringing happiness and contentment to his family. He reasons that the basic purpose for working is to support his demanding family. When his work takes him away from his family, he rationalizes that he is making huge sacrifices to keep his family happy. Somehow he doesn't catch the signals that his family would prefer more of him and less money. Otto, a restaurant owner, expresses the old husband point of view:

"It's hard for an outsider to appreciate how difficult the restaurant business is. The only way a business like this can prosper is for the owner to be married to the restaurant. I wish I had one of those nice comfortable office jobs where you can come home and visit with your family every night after work, but in my business such is not the case. It's work, work, work. An owner must constantly check up to see if the customers are satisfied and that the help is kept on their toes.

"Besides, if I didn't work these long hours, my family would have very little. With the cost of everything being so high, you have to make a large income to raise a family. We would have very few luxuries if I were not a restaurant owner. I make all these sacrifices for my wife and children."

An organization man style of husband is open about the fact that the quest for career advancement is the primary motivating force in his life. A wife and children are valued by an organization man to a large extent because they can help him climb the organizational ladder. Kent, a middle manager in a large conservative company, expresses his views about family vis-à-vis career this way:

"Any manager with political savvy knows that a family helps a manager get ahead as long as they don't put up too much flak. If you are married with children, it's seen as a sign of stability by the company. They also figure that if you have a family you have to keep plugging away at the job. Beyond that, the company assumes a married man won't need to spend so much time and energy chasing after women. Another very practical consideration is that it's convenient to bring a wife to parties given by company executives. If you aren't married, your boss might think you are interested in his wife."

A totally liberated husband has a much less manipulative and exploitative view of the relationship between career and family. He typically feels that work must be held in proper perspective; that work is a constructive force only when it facilitates meaningful relationships with family members. Work is viewed by the totally liberated husband as a means of improving the quality of life. Spencer, a computer programmer, illustrates this point of view.

"I can't personalize the Great American He-Man Dream of pushing for more and more material things. Working forty hours a week can mess up relationships with people. My wife, children, and I need more time with each other than most jobs allow. I work mostly on a subcontract basis. When my family and I need some more money for things, I take on an assignment for this computer firm I'm connected with. The same goes for my wife's work as a free-lance copywriter. We use money for very specific purposes. Chasing career goals is a trip hung on the American male that has done a lot of damage to the quality of life in this country."

The new husband, at his best, skillfully integrates career and family demands. Although he doesn't invariably reach his goal, he attempts to achieve success both on the job and at home. His feeling of inner contentment is highest when his family is happy and his career is throbbing with success. Gene, a principal in a public relations firm, represents the new husband thinking about combining family and career success:

"I try to keep both my career and family in balanced perspective, although it isn't always easy. Last spring I recall having a big client prospect on the hook at the same time my wife was going through a miscarriage. She was depressed and legitimately required a lot of my time and attention. Nevertheless, my prospective client wanted to sign a contract right away for public relations services. Getting things ready for the client demanded a lot of extra hours of work. The way I finally pulled things out of the fire was to explain my predicament to the company that was considering using the services of our firm. I asked the client to postpone his final decision just one week. Then I spent as much time at home as possible during the next week. During my wife's recuperation, she required a lot of sleep. I finished up final details on the project while my wife napped during the day and right after dinner.

"As things worked out, our firm received the valuable contract and my wife didn't feel that I was neglecting her in time of need. She was taking her miscarriage pretty hard, and needed frequent reassurance."

The New Husband as Juggler

A distinguishing characteristic of a wide range of new husbands is their ability to simultaneously do justice to their careers and personal life. Many men who achieve extraordinary success in their careers fall prey to the trap of wrecking their home lives in the process. Men at the bottom of their fields, however, are also often guilty of family neglect. Family desertion and child battering, for example, are found almost exclusively among men of modest accomplishment in the world of work. New husbands, in contrast to the two groups of men just cited, make a continuous effort to insure that their own career pursuits do not deteriorate the quality of personal relationships at home. At the same time, the career-minded new husband seems to be able to prevent the comforts of family life from slowing down his career progress.

Barry, a dynamic and likeable person, was the vice-president of marketing at a Long Island company. An executive placement firm approached Barry with the opportunity of becoming president of a company located near Chicago. Ecstatic about the prospects of taking over the presidency of a company of substantial size, Barry discussed the job offer at home. Nan, his wife, thought the possibility sounded intriguing and welcomed the opportunity to leave the congestion of Long Island behind. She felt that once located in Chicago, she could readily find new employment as a registered nurse.

David and Carol, Barry's children, bemoaned the prospects of relocation. David reasoned that transferring a high school student during the beginning of his senior year was about as considerate as sending him to prison. Carol shared David's sentiments, noting that she was entering her last year of junior high school. Accepting the feelings of his children, although not totally agreeing with them, Barry decided to explore this intriguing new position further.

After three exploratory trips to the Chicago company, Barry was offered the presidency effective whenever he could gracefully leave his present job. While in flight from Chicago to New York, Barry drew up a package deal to sell his family. Calling for a family conference, Barry had a unique proposition to offer Nan, David, and Carol:

"Okay gang, let me tell you the whole story before you all jump ship. The job at Ramco is extraordinary. Aside from being given a chance to run an exciting company, my annual income, if things go well, will be about $65,000 per year—much better than I'm doing now. I'll even be able to send my children to college without my having to tend bar at night.

"But I recognize that this move couldn't be more poorly timed. If I were entering my last year of school, I would probably run away from home before relocating. My plans are to actually commute to this job from now until the end of the school year. I'll take all my vacation days by staying in Long Island for ten consecutive Fridays once May rolls around.

"I'll take the 7 P.M. flight from JFK to Chicago on Sunday nights. My plans are to come back on the 2:30

P.M. flight every Friday from O'Hare to JFK. I'll get most of my extra paper work done in flight, and I'll have the entire weekend to spend with my family, assuming seniors still want to spend time with their father. Maybe when David looks around for a college, he could choose one in the Midwest. I know he's been talking favorably about Big Ten Schools for a while anyway. Now if you folks buy my package deal, maybe the company will bear with a long-distance commuter for a president until midsummer."

Nan, David, Carol, and the board of directors at Ramco all bought Barry's proposition. As things have worked out, the whole family adjusted favorably to Chicago as home, and Barry is doing very well as a company president.

A commendable characteristic about many new husbands is their ability to make concessions to their family, yet still do justice to their careers. New husbands tend to rise to the top of situations even when they undergo a dramatic shift in their usual way of life. Craig's situation is an ideal example of many new husbands' flexibility and resourcefulness.

Similar to thousands of other middle managers and executives commuting to New York from the suburbs on a daily basis, Craig was searching for a new life style. A normal work day would find Craig leaving his Stamford, Connecticut, home at 7:15 in the morning and returning approximately twelve hours later. Unlike many other commuters, however, Craig was not naive about how managers in smaller towns arrange their work schedules. Craig explains:

"My work as a financial analyst for the company gets me around to many of our plants. In small towns, the management team actually spends much more time at work than a commuter does. My colleagues and I in New

York waste a couple of hours per day. Sure, you can recapture some of the time spent in commuting by reading the newspaper or taking care of some office paper work, but there is still a lot of slippage in time. It's not unusual on a snowy day to arrive in the office about 10:00 in the morning after having left the house around 7:00. The time you spend standing around waiting for delayed trains, being squashed during the subway ride, and driving your car from the train station to your house is all wasted.

"Your counterpart in a small town at least has a choice. He arrives at the office at 8 A.M. and leaves at 6:00 sometimes just to look good to his boss. But, if he wants, he can leave the house at 8:30 and return by 5:00, having put in a good solid day of work. A commuter has no choice. You have to spend hours per day being breathed and coughed upon by a mass of humanity. The whole process is ludicrous. Besides, my analysis suggests that a commuter to New York spends about 250 dollars per month for the privilege of commuting. My figure includes only those costs that go beyond the amounts of money you might spend for going to work in a small town. You have to figure in the cost of executive lunches, the clothing that wears out so fast because of the constant cleaning required, the dinners and hotels in the city when you miss the last train, the cab rides, the parking fee for keeping your car in the railroad station parking lot, and lastly those ever increasing commuter train tickets. The whole thing is organized lunacy."

Craig found an elegant solution to his problems. An ambitious individual, he searched for a life style that would challenge him professionally, provide enough money for himself, his wife, and two children to live comfortably, and—most importantly—give him more time to spend with his family. Craig had come to believe that his present life style was remarkably inefficient. Although his gross income was high, much of it was dissipated by the high cost of living in the New York metropolitan area. A large proportion of his time at home was spent recuperating from fatigue caused by the strain of commuting. After months of careful planning, Craig hit upon the idea of becoming a community college teacher in a small town. In addition he would work as a free-lance income tax consultant.

"Having an M.B.A. degree was a big asset to me in my search for the right setup. After some digging into the prospects of finding a teaching position at a community college, I quickly learned that hundreds of active businessmen and retired executives were searching for the same job. It didn't dissuade me from at least giving it a try. All I needed was one job. I mailed out my resume to about fifty two-year colleges and followed up each with a phone call. I was shocked when one of my routine phone calls resulted in an invitation for a job interview. Anna, the children, and I drove up to Bangor, Maine, that weekend so we could look over the area and take care of my job interview. To my astonishment, I was offered a job as an assistant professor of accounting at $13,000 per year.

"We bought a fine old house on the edge of the city for $23,000, having sold my home in Stamford—with less room—for $67,500. I was left with a nifty cash profit of close to $12,000. My wife and children were jubilant at the prospects of living together as a united family. Good-bye to long commuting trips and frequent visits to out-of-town plants. I converted one room of our house into an office, and hung up a shingle 'Private Tax Consultant.' Within four months I had all the business I needed. It was a blast helping farmers out with problems like finding the right depreciation schedules for silos, and advising them whether or not their children's labor can be called a business expense. By the end of one year in Maine, I was grossing about $18,000 and only working an average of 45 to 50 hours per week.

"What I enjoyed most from a financial angle is that we were living better in Bangor on $18,000 than we were in Stamford on close to $30,000. Our life together as a family was also enriched. I finally had the chance to attend Cub and Brownie meetings. Anna has escaped all those volunteer activities in Stamford that were taking up her time, but providing her with negative satisfaction. She's now trying to develop some patterns for do-it-yourself ski outfits that she hopes to begin marketing next year. Her requirements for becoming a creative, contributing person in addition to being a homemaker are now being met. Our transition from Stamford to Bangor hasn't been trouble free, but it's apparent to me that the general direction of our life is now upstream."

Wives and Children Are Career Helpers

Many husbands, particularly old husbands and organization men, find negative or indirect reasons why a family helps a man's career. Often their emphasis is upon reasons that are uncomplimentary to their families. For example, one husband told me that his wife and children help his career along because "They cost me so much money, I have to work hard just to survive. Without them around I might relax too much." Even more cynically, an engineer volunteered, "Without a wife and child, I'd spend most of my time chasing women instead of improving myself professionally."

New husbands, in contrast, see their wives and children (if any) as making a positive contribution to their careers. Instead of working hard to avoid the consequences of not working hard (such as nonpayment of bills incurred by the family), the new husband feels that his family enhances his career involvement. The implication is not to be drawn that, without a wife or other form of exclusive relationship, a new husband would abandon his career, but that a good relationship fortifies career interests.

George D. Bertolet, a photographic technician, expresses simply and genuinely how marriage helps his career: "It helps to have someone who cares about you and is willing to discuss your problems with you." Marty, a broker in a real estate investment firm, elaborates upon the *caring* theme:

"Right now I'm working on the biggest real estate deal of my life. A major bank in our area is trying to sell a new office building they own for $40,000,000. Our firm has landed the contract to negotiate this sale and I've been given the assignment. It's filled with excitement and intrigue. You don't just put a classified ad in the local paper saying 'Like-new twenty story office building for sale. Asking price $40,000,000, with only $10,000,000 down; carpeted throughout.'

"I rushed outside of my office to tell my secretary of this coup. All she could say was 'That'll keep you busy for a while.' If I tell a friend at lunch, he would probably respond by telling me about a big deal that his firm is about to undertake. When you tell friends about your successes or almost successes, they tend to ignore you or try to top you.

"At home, the situation is much different. Molly couldn't be more pleased than if she landed the deal herself. Molly is also a real estate person, but she deals mostly with residential property. She prepared shrimp creole—my favorite meal—to celebrate my getting the assignment of negotiating the building sale. Alice and Hugh, our two children, were also enthusiastic about the deal. Both agreed they would like to take a trip downtown to ride the elevators on the building before I sell it. Hugh wanted to know if I would have to give away any of the $40,000,000 if I sold the building. Alice planned to ask her social studies teacher if the class could arrange a field trip to inspect the building.

"That incident, more than any other in my career, made me realize that my wife and children really care what I'm up to. It's a terrific feeling to experience in this cold, competitive world. Maybe not every man is so fortunate, but I am, and it helps keep me going in bad times."

A number of married males have told me and my researchers that marriage and children provide a forward thrust to their careers because it makes the effort seem worthwhile. Although plenty of unattached people are able to gain forward momentum in their careers, an attached individual—and families unequivocally make a man feel attached—finds ready justification for his labors. Charles D. Curran, a reimbursement supervisor in Virginia, expresses the opinion that a wife and children help a man's career because, "To be interested and to share gives purpose and a feeling that it is worth the effort." Gary, a purchasing agent at a college, extends this reasoning further:

"I've taken courses in industrial psychology and I know that work is supposed to have some powerful lure in itself. I guess if I took all those theories about work motivation seriously, buying supplies for my college would be the most important thing in the world to me. But who can really claim that buying paper toweling and floor wax in large quantities is his mark on the world? Work is kicks, and I enjoy making deals with suppliers to help control costs at our college. I even attend a buyer's seminar now and then.

"At the end of a month, it's kind of hard for me to

pinpoint what it is that I've actually accomplished. If I were an architect, I would have some tangible evidence that I was doing something important. But, in my job, I sometimes wonder if my salary can really be justified. Maybe I could be replaced with two part-time college students who could do my job just as well, and yet be paid the minimum wage. When I'm feeling close to my wife and child, I don't need to find all kinds of complicated meaning in my work. Having a wife and a child who need your love and attention, and a few dollars besides, is reason enough for working.

"I have a little trick that I've developed to help me get through the dullest committee meeting at work. When somebody is rambling away just to look good to the rest of the group, I let my mind wander and think about all the good times the three of us have together."

Yet another career benefit some new husbands derive from family life is a feeling of confidence in their work stemming from a warm home situation. Being loved and accepted helps bolster self-confidence in general, and the area of work is no exception. Andrew P. Davis, a manager in the chain restaurant business, states, "If a man gets his feeling of confidence from a warm home he will do better in all things. Of course, if the home is cold and unfriendly, his career will suffer."

New husbands and old husbands alike in responsible positions frequently rely upon the listening skills of their wives to assist them in solving business and professional problems. This "executive confidante" role has come somewhat into disfavor in recent years because of its implication that the husband *uses* his wife as a sounding board. Nevertheless, management consultants are hired by many buisness firms at several hundred dollars a day just to listen to executives talk about work-related problems. Henry, a marketing executive, explains how his wife helps him in his career by acting as an executive confidante:

"Lucy and I help each other with our careers. Lucy is a dress designer for a garment manufacturer. I'm in charge of marketing for a paper box company. When I'm wrestling with a thorny problem, such as whether or not to fire a particular employee, I talk out loud about the problem with Lucy. She listens sympathetically and often confronts me with some of the inconsistencies in my thinking. Most of all, Lucy is a terrific listener. When you're a vice president, it's hard to find a good listener at work. So many people are playing political games, they can't listen objectively.

"I try to listen as effectively to Lucy as she listens to me. Even when she is mulling over a technical problem such as whether or not to recommend one dress design over another, I listen attentively. Even if I don't know too much about dress design, I can at least tell Lucy when I don't think her logic is convincing."

Career Progress Often Helps a Marriage

Gloom peddlers are quick to point out that career success is usually associated with a diminished quality of home life—particularly when the success is both substantial and sudden. Easily cited are case histories of astronauts, novelists, and heart transplant surgeons whose sudden acceleration to nationwide prominence was followed shortly by a breakup of their marriage. Although nationwide success and its coincident time demands can play havoc with a stable home situation, my observations are that in many instances career success actually helps a marriage. A new husband rarely uses worldly success as a rationalization for creating problems at home. Angelo, an involved and caring husband and father, finally made it big in the construction business. His small firm became the prime contractor for a city-owned ramp garage. Tina, his wife, explains what happened:

"Ange has always been a solid father and husband. He has forever worked long hours at full steam. I had more confidence in him than he had in himself. I knew that his honest way of doing business would someday have a big payoff. No under the table or payola deals for Ange's outfit. He had a reputation for honest business practices. Our biggest problem together was that Ange worried too much about business. He was forever concerned that he wouldn't be able to finance college for the children or that I wouldn't have enough money to open the boutique shop I had been planning for years. Ange, for all his good points, is one to brood over business problems.

"Then things went well in a hurry for Ange and his partners. The ramp garage contract just about doubled our income. Instead of spending extra hours at work to manage the new contract, Ange hired a site manager. His good performance led to another lucrative contract for Ange's firm. The better things went for Ange, the closer he became to the children and me. Instead of fretting so much, he smiled much more. I could see some of the wrinkles disappearing from his face. Ange began to remember more of the things that brought us so much happiness in the early years of our marriage. Annoying little mistakes, like the telephone company charging us for long distance calls we never made, didn't seem to bother Ange as much as they did in the past.

"We always had a good relationship, but now Ange was able to express more of his love. The children could also see the difference. I'm hoping that Ange's giant success continues both for his sake, for me, and the children."

John E. Tropman, professor of social work at the University of Michigan, has contributed some findings suggesting that career success is associated with more stable marriages. "The conventional wisdom is that the hard driving type executive forsakes all for his job," said Tropman in an interview with Gannett News Service. "In the main, that turns out not to be true. Our findings reverse the assumption that upward mobility causes family instability."

Tropman's findings are based on the job progress of about 6,000 males between the ages of forty-five and fifty-four. Although the basic information contained in his report is based upon data from the 1962 Census, the general trend it presents seems still relevant today. Men in this study who progressed the farthest were those who had remained married to their first wives. Second in the rate of career advancement were those men who had been remarried. Far behind, Tropman notes, are men who had been divorced, separated, or who had become widowers.

Easing the Relocation Trauma

New husbands have become sensitive to the possible adverse impact of geographic relocation upon family happiness. A distinct trend has emerged whereby new husbands either refuse to relocate or, as in the case of Barry discussed earlier, try hard to ease the transition for their families. *Business Week* found that an increasing number of young executives refuse relocation if they think it will interfere with family welfare and the "good life." Management psychologist Harry Levinson observes, "People are asking themselves, 'What am I going to get out of it?' The sentiment goes along with hippies questioning life styles, kids questioning their parents."

Included in family welfare, of course, is an increasing concern about the negative effects of relocation upon both the well-being of the children and the wife's career. Rodney, an executive in the publishing business, reflects these dual concerns in his comments about why he turned down an attractive job offer:

"A splendid opportunity came along for me to become managing editor of a small educational publisher. There was more money in it than I am making now but, more important than that, it was the kind of responsibility I was seeking. I turned it down because the timing was so bad. My wife and child had just gotten over the 'wooly woolies' from our last move two years ago. Dorothy, my wife, had just been promoted to office manager in the insurance agency where she worked. Our child, Phil, had really come to enjoy life in our new neighborhood.

"It's not that my family calls all the shots about where we live, but I think we've been through enough relocation for a while. Dorothy deserves her recent promotion and office manager jobs are not easy to come by when a woman changes communities. Maybe I'll get another chance to become a managing editor at a later date. For now, keeping the family ship floating smoothly seems more important."

The widespread attention given to the possible ill effects of relocation upon a family has led many husbands to share the responsibility with their wives for easing the relocation trauma. Moving is not inevitably traumatic, according to MIT sociologist Herbert J. Gans and others who have seriously studied the problem. When husbands and wives share the tasks required to soften the impact of geographic relocation, adjustment to the move is facilitated. Tom, a personnel manager (and a new husband type himself) notes that, "When an executive relocates in our company, his first assignment is to stay home and help his wife and children adjust to the move. Our policy may be paternalistic, but it works. A family that works the bugs out of a move at the outset is much more likely to want to stay in the community. An executive who's harassed because his wife and children are climbing the walls of their new home is not a very productive member of the management team."

An intriguing study by sociologist Stella B. Jones, reported in the *Journal of Marriage and the Family*, analyzes the mechanisms that help people adjust to a new community. All of these "mechanisms" are specific things that a husband and wife should take care of in order to ease the relocation burden. In the past, housewives have been assigned most of these tasks. The new husband does what he can to share these chores, tasks, and responsibilities. According to Ms. Jones, the twelve most helpful mechanisms for facilitating adjustment to a new community are:[1]

- Arrival of furniture and other familiar objects
- Return to "normal" schedule
- Meeting neighbors in the new neighborhood
- Arrival of newspapers
- Familiar chain stores, restaurants, brands
- Watching favorite family TV programs
- Helpful real estate agents
- Letters from friends
- Letters from relatives
- Friendly, helpful co-workers of the husband
- Locating friends in new community known prior to moving there
- Presence of family pets

New Husbands Do Not Feel Oppressed

"We, as men, want to take back our full humanity. We no longer want to strain to compete to live up to an impossible oppressive masculine image—strong, silent, cool, handsome, unemotional, master of women, leader of men, wealthy, brilliant, athletic, and 'heavy.' We no longer want to feel the need to perform sexually, socially, or in any way live up to an imposed male role, from a traditional American society or a 'counterculture.'"

Words such as these quoted from the Berkeley Men's

Center Manifesto—a collective of men struggling to free themselves from sex-role stereotypes and to define themselves in positive, nonchauvinistic ways—are hardly the battle cry of the new husbands. In contrast, members of the Berkeley Men's Center feel that the American male is oppressed, as do many totally liberated husbands.

Warren Farrell, regarded by some as the leader of the movement for male liberation in the United States, has done much to publicize what he sees as pressures placed upon males. Totally liberated husbands would agree with Farrell's opinions, while new husbands tend to feel much less restricted or oppressed. His opinions are worth noting here because of the contrast they make with the attitudes of new husbands. Farrell reports on the kinds of concerns married and single middle-aged males express in consciousness raising groups:

"Middle age is when men realize how the male mystique has been hurting them. They're on the corporate ladder and know they aren't going to make it to the top in middle age—or else they may even fall off. They think they've been working all their lives as a way of showing love for their families. In middle age they find they don't know how to express love to wife or children. . . .

"A society that makes 'success objects' out of men keeps men in the rat race. This success object—win the game, bring home the bacon—role is just as unfair to men as the success-object role thrust upon women."

He further notes that the destructiveness of the success-object role is not so visible. Chasing after success can make a man race directly to the grave, never having time to know or be what he wants to be. New husbands, in contrast, are proud of their masculine role and generally content with their life style. John, a lawyer in upstate New York, explains why he doesn't find his role in life confining or oppressive:

"I enjoy my situation in life in relation to my wife, children, and career. Being a successful lawyer and a good husband and father makes me feel masculine. I do not see myself as a sexist for making that statement. Perhaps a woman would feel more feminine if she were a successful lawyer, mother, and wife. Whatever the case, I enjoy feeling masculine even if I'm not exactly sure what the term masculine means.

"Do I feel harassed because I have to go to work, day in and day out to make a living? No, my work gives meaning to my life. I'm just not the type to philosophize my days away and do odd jobs just to pay for the necessities in life. In some ways, I think I use my family as an excuse for working hard. If I only had to pay for my own way in life, I wouldn't have too many good answers for the inevitable question about why I work so hard. Furthermore, I'm not entirely convinced that working hard for a living is particularly a male role. Some people enjoy working hard and would find a difficult job to do even if society thought they should be staying at home. We have had hard driving career women throughout the entire United States history. My mother was both a flapper and an advertising executive.

"Yes, we definitely have specific sex roles in our household and I enjoy the tasks assigned to me by sex. My wife is a strong 105 pounder with good solid shoulders, legs, and arms, but I discourage her from changing flat tires. I've been changing car wheels since I was twenty years old so can do the job much more safely. The other day it was 15 degrees outside and the snow was blowing. Roz, my wife, came in the house with a 'damsel in distress' look on her face to tell me she had a flat tire. Of course, I was the one to change the tire. I'll risk being called a sexist at the expense of my wife being conked on the chin by a recalcitrant bumper jack. Sometimes the neighborhood dogs are quite unfriendly with the kinds of souvenirs they leave on our lawn. And that's about the most oppressive task assigned to the male role in our family—cleaning up dog manure."

Ambitious New Husbands Create Some Problems

Despite the overall picture of strength and sensitivity presented of new husbands in this book, they are not angelic all of the time. Undoubtedly, new husbands are more responsive to the demands of their wives and children than are old husbands, but totally liberated husbands might be more responsive than new husbands. New husbands who are ambitious with respect to their careers sometimes allow these ambitions to create some problems at home. An avid pursuit of success and responsiveness to spouse and children are not always compatible, despite the general tendency of success to foster good family relationships.

Preoccupation with work is the prime villain in regard to creating problems at home for the ambitious new husband. An incident I reported in my book, *Women in Transition,* represents a classic example of how a busy person who perhaps genuinely cares about his (or her) family may be temporarily unresponsive because of preoccupation with job matters:

> Dr. Elliot Burns, a physician and hospital administrator, has a meeting the next day with the hospital board of trustees in order to seek approval for physical expansion of the hospital. Cynthia, his wife, has just learned that Wendy, their youngest daughter, has slipped from the middle to the bottom reading group in the fourth grade. Cynthia initiates conversation about the reading problem and spends five minutes presenting all the details as relayed to

> her by the teacher and Wendy. Elliot responds, "Yeah, that's interesting."
>
> Cynthia interprets his response as symptomatic of his preoccupation with work and consequent neglect of important family matters. Elliot interprets this conversation from a different point of view. His interpretation is "How can Cynthia bother me with Wendy's fourth-grade reading problem when I'm facing an eleven million dollar decision tomorrow?"[2]

A characteristic of ambitious people—even new husbands—is that their moods are often directly influenced by events related to their career. A new husband facing a critical business or professional problem may be emotionally down because of that situation. His relationship with his wife or children may be going quite well and yet he might respond to them in a withdrawn, distant manner. Why is this different from the proverbial husband who takes out his job frustrations by yelling at his wife and children? The major difference is that the ambitious husband is more emotionally tied to his job than is his less ambitious counterpart. An ambitious husband who learns he has been passed over for promotion is going to stay discouraged or depressed much longer than the unambitious man who is angered because he was unable to find a good parking space that morning.

Pam, a high school English teacher and free-lance copy editor, is married to Brian, a prosecuting attorney. She describes what she sees as the biggest problem in their relationship, and Brian does not disagree: "Brian is a first-rate husband. Our relationship now is as good as it was during the two years we lived together. Our big problem, as I see it, is that Brian's moods are more influenced by his work than by me. If he has won a big case, there is nothing I can do that will annoy him. After a big win in the courtroom, Brian smiles most of the time and has unlimited energy for everything. It works for him even if I'm in somewhat of a bitchy mood myself.

"On the other hand, if Brian is in the doldrums because of a political hassle or some other catastrophe about his job, he just doesn't seem to respond to anything positive about our relationship. One Valentine's day I invited him out to our favorite Mexican restaurant. He sulked most of the evening because it looked as if an alleged murderer he was prosecuting would not be convicted. Brian wasn't insulting—he never is. What concerned me is that Brian couldn't get emotionally up for this special night I had arranged."

Resentment is yet another problem sometimes created by successful husbands, even if they happen to be new husbands. This resentment is most likely to surface in relationships where one spouse is getting far more satisfaction from work than his or her partner. In a traditional nuclear family arrangement this resentment is likely to occur when the husband has an exciting job while the wife is simultaneously dissatisfied with her role as homemaker or her job. An embarrassing example of this type of resentment was made public at a cocktail party attended by people from a diverse group of employers. In response to an inquiry about his line of work, one man mentioned that he was a manager of information systems. He was then asked what it is that a person with such an impressive sounding job title does. Before he could answer, his wife volunteered, "Don't let him impress you with his title. He's really the chief errand boy for the company president."

Fortunately most new husbands (plus totally liberated ones) and their wives have sound enough relationships whereby feelings of resentment can be openly discussed. A wife of a new husband who felt such resentment would be able to say to her spouse, "Something is bothering me, I can't help resenting the fact that you have a much more exciting life than I do." He, in turn, would probably respond, "Okay, let's talk some more about *our* problem." Perhaps this is the essential difference between a new husband and an old husband or a *new* relationship and an *old* relationship.

chapter 7

His and Her Career

Two very special people are required to manage a dual-career family—a nontraditional wife and a new or liberated husband. Any family in which the husband and wife (or a live-together couple) both work is not necessarily a dual-career family. The big difference lies in the words *dual* and *career*. In this arrangement both the male and female have jobs into which each invests considerable time and emotional energy. Instead of just working for a living, each partner feels that he or she has a life-long commitment to work—the difference between a job and a career. Duality is involved because both have approximately equal professions, in terms of status and/or income. A marital team in which the husband is an otolaryngologist and the wife is a bank clerk is not a true dual-career family. However, if the same ear, nose, and throat doctor were married to a cardiologist, that would be a dual-career family.

Couples with his and her careers are somewhat more frequent than couples with his and her Rolls Royces, but they are still not abundant. Perhaps one family in a hundred in which both the husband and wife work can truly be considered a dual-career family. Many more dual-career families will be found in the future as more women have access to bigger jobs. Looking into some of the problems and opportunities created by this emerging life style is valuable because it sheds additional insight into the psyche of the nontraditional husband. Also, even if the husband and wife may not have equally big jobs, they both will face *some* of the problems experienced by a dual-career family.

Competitive Feelings

Feelings of competitiveness between husband and wife about each other's career often exist even when one of the marital partners happens to be a new husband. The totally liberated male professes to be free of the male *machismo* dictating that males must outperform females, yet some feelings of competitiveness are almost inevitable when two ambitious people are emotionally involved with each other. Competitive feelings are all the more likely to surface when the husband and wife are engaged in approximately the same kind of work.

Dan and his common-law wife, Lois, were both graduate teaching assistants at a midwestern university. They entered graduate school at the same time, but Lois received her Ph.D. one year before Dan. Within days after having finished her requirements for the degree, other members of the psychology department realized that Lois had completed her degree first. Good naturedly, a younger graduate student said upon greeting them, "Good morning Dr. and Mr. Vernon." Dan levels about how he felt:

"I pride myself on having a very equal and a very open relationship with Lois. But that comment hurt. I recall blushing and feeling very uncomfortable. Of course, I was happy for Lois's success, but the feeling of having lost out in competition with her was almost a reflex reaction. We graduated from college together and shortly thereafter entered graduate school as somewhat of a team. We took many of our classes together. It just never occurred to me that Lois would get her degree before me, and I never gave any thought to how I would feel if it did occur. I think I've matured considerably since that incident, but I would not say that we have lost all of our feelings of competitiveness between us.

"We are both doing research in the area of nonverbal communication these days. We have even collaborated on a couple of studies. Nevertheless, Lois starts acting just a little jealous if I get an article published in a better journal than she does. Last year Lois was invited to become a member of a select scientific committee, and I wasn't. It was then my turn to feel pangs of envy.

"We plan to do a book on nonverbal communication someday. Our present thinking is to toss a coin to see who will be the senior author. Maybe what's blocking us from moving forward on that project is that we're both afraid that we might lose the coin toss. One suggestion Lois had would be to indicate on the book jacket how the senior author was chosen. I know this would be an academic book, but putting 'Senior author chosen by a toss of the coin' would look bizarre. No matter what the rationale, I would still prefer not to be my wife's junior author. And I don't blame Lois; she wouldn't want to be junior author either."

Dr. Lynda Lytle Holmstrom reports in her book, *The Two-Career Family,* that most of the twenty dual-career couples she studied did not find feelings of competitiveness to constitute a problem. The general case in a dual-career family is for one person to accelerate past the other in career progress. Holmstrom reports the comments of a husband who does not feel competitive with his wife although she has moved past him in her career.

> There's never been any competition. . . . I mean we don't look at it this way . . . I suppose I could feel embarrassed if I wanted to, but it isn't going to change anything to feel embarrassed. Sure I'd like to be able to equal it but I can't, and I never will, and I know I can't. I'm not going to waste my time wishing I could . . . I don't think we're of that nature. . . . We are never competing for anything I can think of over the other, if you follow what I mean.[1]

Dual-career couples who feel the most competitive sometimes cope with these feelings by eventually avoiding activities that throw them into the most open competition—such as joint ventures. Rather than weaken a relationship, the couple opts to run their careers on different tracks. Comments from a wife's interview, reported by Holmstrom, illustrate how situations evoking competitive strivings sometimes come to be avoided by a dual-career family.

> I think there's always been competition. One relates a little differently to one's other colleagues than one does to one's spouse. We once tried writing something together and that was disastrous. . . . We just took the necessary argumentation personally. . . . We do not count one another's publications or anything like that. It's rather a question of more subtle things. It's a question of how you relate to others in your community and each other's

> community. Just for example, my husband absolutely refuses to be regarded as (Mary Smith's) husband. (laughter) I'm supposed to be his wife. And for that reason, he doesn't enjoy being in company which is primarily associated with me. . . . And if we have joint acquaintances, as we do, then he's very sort of sensitive to this kind of thing.[2]

The husband just described may in reality be more of a traditional than a new or liberated husband. Nevertheless, even a new husband may have a few blind spots about his sexist attitudes—such as not wanting to be known as the husband of ______ .

Colleagueship

The highest form of dual-career families involves husbands and wives who act as colleagues to each other. Few couples are able to accomplish this feat, but, when it works, it can be a source of life-long pleasure to the new husband and his wife. William H. Masters and Virginia E. Johnson have served as a model for hundreds of other male-female teams of sex therapists around the country. In sessions with clients or patients, these teams typically mesh rather than compete. A new husband and sex therapist from Pennsylvania describes the colleague relationship between him and his wife:

"First of all, you couldn't go into something as sensitive as sex therapy if the man and woman were trying to work out their own power drives in front of the patients. We work together as life partners and professional partners. Nora offers me criticism of what she observes in the sessions and I do likewise for her. The other day she told me that I was bearing down too heavy on a man telling him not to look for physical causes for his impotence.

Nora said the man just wasn't ready for a psychological explanation of his difficulties. She was probably right. The unique thing about our relationship, in comparison to the hundreds of couples we observe in our practice, is that we don't play tit for tat. I don't now offer Nora a constructive criticism because she offered me one."

As valuable as technical advice might be from a colleague, the emotional support possible from such a relationship might be even more valuable. Emotional support is obviously not the exclusive province of a colleaguelike marital relationship, but encouragement from a person whose professional opinion is respected is particularly helpful when professional matters are involved. Liz and Carl, married co-owners of an employment agency in Chicago, give each other emotional support whenever it is needed. Carl explains:

"Before telling you how Liz and I feed each other emotional support, you have to understand why a person in this business needs emotional support. Our business cycle resembles a roller coaster. When business is booming, we have lots of jobs to offer but we have to scramble around for qualified applicants. Most of the good applicants get swooped up pretty quickly in good times. When the economy starts to slip, even before a real crunch hits business, the number of assignments from business and industry begins to taper off. Then the applicants flock to our doors. We have to turn away some top-flight people who are exploring the possibilities of advancing their careers.

"During the last business downturn, I must have had 100 people from the machine tool industry make legitimate inquiries about finding new employment. I was afraid that, when I needed good applicants again, our agency would have developed the reputation of being unable to place people in that field. Liz came to my rescue and helped me put things in proper perspective. She explained that my sincere, helpful approach to job applicants would win them back when times were good again. Her encouragement came at the right time. It sure beats popping Valium as a way to cope with the rigors of this business.

"When I sense that Liz needs some bolstering, I try to step in and tell her about her good points. One pushy client was leaning on Liz contending that she wasn't trying hard enough to find him a few women engineers. I told her not to worry because the guy was panicking because the company was five years behind the times in their recruiting efforts for professional women."

Time Is a Precious Resource

Finding enough time to spend with each other, with the child or children (if the couple has children of their own), and with the demands of a career is a major problem confronting dual-career families. Considerable sensitivity toward each other's problems and mutual respect for each other's work is required to prevent time pressures from playing havoc with a dual-career couple's relationship. Kent, a professor of economics and college department head, is married to a child psychologist, Flora. Married to each other relatively late in life, they have one child—three-year-old Amy. Kent's description of a typical Thursday provides a glimpse into the problems of time management faced by the dual-career family:

"The alarm rings at 7:15, much to the chagrin of Flora and me. It's my day to get Amy ready for the day care center, so I hop out of bed first. First thing I do is to run into Amy's room to kiss her good morning and flip her an orange to keep her busy until I'm ready to help her get dressed. I use the downstairs bathroom with the miniature TV in it so I can watch the 'Today Show' while shaving. Amy interrupts those ten minutes of planned tranquility with a detailed account of a bad dream about a 'Good Humor' man who turned out to be a devil.

"By 8:00 I'm dressed. Then I finish dressing Amy who has contributed something to the effort by putting on her underwear and one sock. Flora has prepared breakfast that morning since I'm in charge of Amy. Breakfast is from 8:15 until 8:40. Although Amy has squeezed the jelly from her jelly doughnut onto the floor, requiring a quick wipe-up operation, I'm able to get in about twelve minutes of the local paper. Flora has to be to the clinic (her office) by 9:00, so she leaves at 8:30.

"Amy and I leave at 8:45, and I drop her at the day care center by 9:00. My staff meeting is at 9:30, which gives me ten minutes alone in my office to finish the newspaper—a must for an economics professor. My day is filled with the usual routine of a department head: listening to faculty complaints, student complaints, reviewing two proposals for new courses, and attending at least one feckless committee meeting. I leave my office on campus at 4:15 to pick up Amy at 4:30. Back home by 4:45, I shower and change so I can at least look fresh and alert for my Thursday night seminar. Amy watches TV while I have a brief snack. This gives me at least fifteen minutes to digest some of the *Wall Street Journal* along with my meal.

"Reliable Flora pops in at 5:30, just in time to free me up to head off to the campus. Amy and she go off for a brief walk before dinner. Home by around 9, Flora and I have the rest of the evening to ourselves. In the interim between Amy's bedtime and my return home, Flora has been able to take care of some office paper work. On nights when we are both home early, we usually take care of our household chores and professional reading. Now that I've revised my textbook, I'm taking at least a year off from any research or writing. My mental health could stand a little slack in my schedule for a while."

Dual-career families have another problem of time management that few one-career families would think constitutes a problem—when to schedule vacations. Gabe, a city official, and his wife, Jill, a local television producer, have this problem even though they have no children. Jill describes their peculiar problem this way: "Vacations are important to Gabe and me. We both like to travel and prefer to travel together. An unfortunate thing is that we rarely can find a week that we can both take off at the same time. Gabe's plant shuts down every year at a time that is very inconvenient for me to take off because of a tight programming schedule. He doesn't like to pull rank at his job and be arbitrary about taking a different vacation schedule from lower ranking executives in his plant. As things work out now, most of our vacations together are long weekends."

Closely related to the issue of time as a precious resource is the delicate problem of whose time is more valuable—the man's or the woman's? A traditional couple would automatically assign more value to the man's time; a totally liberated husband and his wife would regard each other's time as having equal value; a new husband and his wife, however, would carefully assess each situation. Eric, an attorney, describes his experiences with the classic catastrophe that often faces a dual-career family with a preschool child:

"It was one of those days you just knew something would go wrong. A carton of milk fell on the floor when Michelle opened the refrigerator. I discovered that I was out of fresh razor blades and had to retrieve a rusty old one from the back of the razor blade dispenser. At 7:45 in the morning we received a phone call from our baby-sitter that she had a severe attack of gastroenteritis and would not be able to come over that day. After six hurried phone calls it appeared we could do nothing until a baby-sitting agency we knew about opened for business. That would probably mean the best we could do was to have Scott safely with a baby-sitter by around noon.

"Perhaps a little bit insensitively, I said to Michelle that she would have to stay home until noon, because I had a house closing at my office at 10:00 in the morning. She retorted, 'Absolutely not. I'm giving an exam at that same hour, and it's just as important as your house closing. Tell somebody else in your firm to handle the closing. There's nobody I can ask at this hour to give the exam for me. Besides, I have the exams with me, so an arrangement like that just couldn't be made. Do I hear you saying that your clients and your work are more important than my work and my students?'

"Darn it, that's exactly what I was saying, and I meant it. I guess I have always attached more importance to legal work than to college teaching. Maybe I was wrong, but time was too limited for philosophizing about the relative values of different kinds of work. My solution, which Michelle bought with a victorious grin on her face, was to have a house closing attended by myself, my client, the opposing attorney and his client, and four-year-old Scott. Being a flexible tyke—a trait he learned from me—Scott kept himself busy in the storeroom drawing cartoons until just about the point at which the deed was signed. Everybody laughed, and now Scott wants to know when he's going to work with me again instead of staying home with the baby-sitter. What Scott doesn't know is that his next field trip will be to administer a biology exam!"

Money and Housework

Dual-career families represent the ultimate example in the sharing pattern described in an earlier chapter. Because the husband and wife strive for an egalitarian relationship, they typically share housework and expenses. A revealing characteristic about the mentality of two-career families is that they tend to have a less sexist accounting philosophy.

A nonsexist pattern of household accounting arrives at a more honest evaluation of his versus her costs of running a household. An accounting system of this nature would consider, as shared expenses, all expenses required to run a two-career family. For instance, the cost of both the husband's and wife's clothing (why should only a woman's clothing be considered a work-related expense?), expenses for both cars, cost of child care, meals eaten outside the home, professional dues for both couples, and cost of preparation of the income tax using the joint form. A truly two-career, completely sharing couple would apportion total expenses in direct relationship to the partner's income. For instance, if the man made 10 percent more money than the woman, he would pay 10 percent more of the total household costs.

In practice, since it takes an astute accountant to figure out the *real* costs of doing anything, most two-career families develop an informal arrangement of his and her expenses that is roughly parallel to each person's ability to pay. Phrases like "he's the breadwinner in the family," or "she works for pin money" are anathema to the two-career family. LeRoy is a high school principal and his wife is a physician. He describes his income-sharing pattern with his wife in a nutshell: "Since we both make above-average incomes, money is no big hassle in our family. Roxanne and I both save money and we also contribute about evenly to household expenses, including big ticket items like new furniture and vacations."

Goodbye, Ceremonial Spouse

Several years ago a brief article by Judy Syfers, "I Want a Wife," was widely circulated. The sentiment behind this article became the theme of many profeminist jokes. A wife who will assist the husband with his work or social functions upon demand is an invaluable asset to a career person. In a two-career family, a wife is not as readily available to provide supportive services for the husband's work or business-related entertaining. She may very well have functions of her own to look after. Even when she is available, involvement of a wife in a husband's career activities requires careful scheduling. The female member of a dual-career family commented to Dr. Holmstrom about this tight scheduling:

> I usually write out a written schedule of what I'm going to do that day. In fact I have a calendar and it has what I'm going to do that day, and anything I know that's coming is on that calendar. My husband has a similar one because where we have two careers, often times I'm required to attend some functions for him and I have to know about it, and he has to know about what I'm doing, to keep things balanced.[3]

At a deeper level than the scheduling problem is the fact that some career women dislike, or even resent, the "sweet hostess" role imposed upon the wives of successful men in certain fields. The traditional role for "Mrs. Executive" is to be a charming asset to her husband's business entertaining. Few new husbands would even want their wives to be prized by others primarily for their skills as a hostess. Herb, a new husband and business executive, describes his revamped notions about the proper role of an executive's wife:

"Years ago, I shared the fantasy of my superiors about the ideal wife of an executive. You know, the charming hostess with the perpetual smile and aseptic household. Something like a cabinet member's or president's wife. As time went by a lot of things happened to Wendy (his wife) and me. She became the modern-day woman in transition, finding herself becoming more deeply enmeshed in her retailing career. By the time the children were adolescents, Wendy had become a full-fledged buyer in our town's biggest independent retail store. Wendy was never exactly the *Good Housekeeping* type, but by then she definitely became the *Cosmopolitan* version of the lovely career woman.

"A couple of years ago, it hit both Wendy and me that the kind of parties we were giving were all wrong. She was being put into the Mrs. Executive role. I would have members of my staff and their wives over for a quasi-business function of mine. My wife's work in retailing didn't give her any stature in these parties because she was being locked into the role of hostessing my party. We rearranged our social functions. Our invitations became joint invitations. We sprinkled our party with business acquaintances of both Wendy's and mine.

"You ask why we didn't have a party with only Wendy's business contacts? The reasoning is simple. I care as much for being 'The head buyer's husband' as Wendy does for being 'The vice-president for corporate development's wife.' Because I exploited Wendy's talents as a hostess in the past, it doesn't mean that she should retaliate by exploiting me."

As hinted in the case of Herb and Wendy, in a two-career family the husband is also less often asked to engage in ceremonial tasks, those often required of husbands in more traditional families. Since the husband in a two-career family is, by definition, committed to his work, his wife is less likely to ask him to devote time to her business or social activities. A woman lawyer belonged to a citizen's action committee involved in trying to blockade the local gas and electric company from being granted a rate increase. Working on a limited budget, a variety of glamorous and nonglamorous tasks had to be accomplished by volunteers. A booth was to be constructed in a shopping center mall as part of the political action group's publicity campaign. The attorney was asked to get her husband to donate some muscle, wood, and paint to help construct the booth. Said she:

"I can see why you would want me to get another pair of hands to help us construct our booth. But why ask my husband? Our campaign isn't his activity. If we do involve him, let's at least make an appeal to Stan's intellect. Just because he's male it doesn't mean he's willing to give us an afternoon of donkey work for our cause."

The Relocation Dilemma

Professional and managerial people often need to be mobile (or stay put if the situation dictates) in order to advance their careers. What happens when one member of a two-career family wants to relocate and the other prefers to stay put? Traditionally, such relocation decisions are settled in favor of the male. Usually, both relocate and the wife does the best she can to find a comparable position in the next town. One woman who managed a restaurant in one town became a cocktail hostess in another, because that was the best job she could find in that town. She had moved there because of her husband's executive promotion. New husbands and their wives tend to carefully evaluate each relocation possibility on its own merits. Although most relocation decisions favor the male—even in two-career families—the picture is rapidly changing.

Ella was an administrative secretary to a top executive in a business machine company. Her husband worked as a design engineer, earning approximately the same annual income as she. Ella's company announced plans to relocate to another city. Although Ella's job was not classified as a managerial position, her outstanding performance influenced the company to make her a unique offer: A salary increase plus the payment of all moving expenses (including a cash "inconvenience allowance") if she would relocate to the new company headquarters. After two evenings of negotiation with her husband Jeff, the couple decided to accept the attractive offer. Three months after relocation Jeff succeeded in finding a position comparable to the job he had left behind to follow his wife.

Another novel approach to relocation taken by new husbands and their wives is to regard themselves as a "package deal" when the question of relocation arises. Duets of this nature, so far, seem to be concentrated in university and laboratory research positions. A corporate recruiter described to me an interesting situation of this nature:

"Our company, like many large, progressive outfits, has been trying vigorously to recruit women engineers and scientists. One day I came upon the resume of a woman Ph.D. chemist with the right subspecialty. Immediately, I wrote her an encouraging letter, extending an invitation to her to visit our laboratory with all expenses paid. The team of people who met this Dr. Helen Addison were quite impressed. In addition to her excellent credentials she was charming and had a good sense of humor. On this basis we figured she was management material. So we just about made her an offer on the spot; one we would confirm in writing shortly thereafter.

"Dr. Addison explained to us that the matter wasn't all that simple. She had a husband back home who had a career of his own. If she would take a new position, he, too, would have to be given suitable employment. Apparently this was a pact the two of them had worked out for themselves. Mr. Addison did come for job interviews. He had an M.S. in physics in a specialty in which we were mildly interested. As things worked out, we did find him a job in our laboratory. I doubt we would have hired him if he were not part of a package deal, but most package deals have a few strings attached."

A rational approach most two-career families take to career management is to seek employment in a stable, large metropolitan area. Quite often both the new husband and his wife can find a series of challenging positions without having to relocate. As Tony describes his straightforward thinking along these lines: "I'm a very work-oriented person. My career is a big part of my life. As a college professor I have to be willing to jump ship if somebody offers me an exciting research grant if I join them. My wife's career as a scientist is important to her and it's also important to me. That's why we stay in the Boston area. Within a radius of sixty-five miles of where we live, there are numerous employment possibilities for both of us. I don't think that even Los Angeles or New York City has anything comparable.

"Not having to worry about what the other person will do if one is offered a good job out of town eliminates one more big hassle that faces a husband and wife who both take their careers seriously. I know a few couples that work for universities as a team, but it's not a very viable possibility anymore. Very few universities have more than one opening at a time. And there is little hope that any of the big universities will be expanding much for the next decade."

The Long-Distance Commuter

A currently fashionable approach to handling the relocation dilemma is for neither couple to relocate. When one member of the two-career family is fortunate enough to find a fascinating job in a distant city, the solution opted by a small number of couples is for one to become a long-distance commuter. Mary Margaret Bothwell has carefully researched a number of these couples for an article published in *New Woman.* Rob and Ruth Weiner are one such couple described by Ms. Bothwell:

> Ruth is the sort of successful woman who has always been good at everything. Top at school, a first-class degree from a university, a good wife and mother, brilliant in her job. At 34 she has risen to become Chairman of the Chemistry Department at the University of Miami. Her husband is Assistant Professor of Chemistry at the University of Denver. With four girls, aged 14 to 8, they have a rather 1970's style of living arrangement. They commute. Or rather Ruth does.
>
> "The girls rotate," Bob chuckles. "The first year, two of the girls went to Miami and two stayed here. The next year it was three and one. They don't mind. It's a trade-off: skiing for swimming, but Colorado still has the most pull." And that's why Ruth does most of the travelling. She gets to Denver for two extended stays (summer and Christmas), plus all the other major holidays and occasional short visits on the end of business trips.
>
> "Some people think we're completely out of our skulls," he says, "but our commuting marriage isn't all that unusual anymore. . . ."[4]

Kathy and Jim are another couple choosing the weekend marriage in preference to relocation. Mary Bothwell reports:

> She has a super-interesting job as a television newscaster in Chicago; he recently accepted a top job in the Justice Department in Washington. Even if she had wanted to try

> broadcasting in the capital, it would have been tough. "My job is based on recognition by the public. I'd have to start all over again," she explains.
>
> Neither she nor Jim wanted to give up their 100-year-old house in Chicago which they had restored themselves. So they sat down to calculate commuting costs.
>
> After much haggling, they decided to buy a second home in Georgetown and divide the commuting fifty-fifty. (Few two career families, of course, could afford such an exotic solution to the relocation dilemma.)
>
> "One of the biggest problems is loneliness," she admits. "We're both homebodies and like to hole-in in the evenings with music and books. Frankly, I'm surprised that more people haven't criticized our decision. The only two who did were *men*." But Kathy isn't the type who bases her life on what *other* people think. "It's entirely our own affair, and our way of life suits us."
>
> Kathy went on: "We get a tremendous exhilaration anticipating the weekends. We are such romantics now. We hear the same music . . . feel the same beat. It's a grand experience, those weekends. Altogether different from a day-to-day marriage . . . which, I think, dulls romance."
>
> But there is another "but." I gathered from both Jim and Kathy that the plane can cause a hideous hassle and a disappointment . . . if it gets fogged in or if someone misses it.[5]

As is apparent from the two case histories just presented, only a new or totally liberated husband would be able to tolerate such an arrangement. Aside from worrying about the possibility that his wife might be conducting an affair with another man, an old husband would require more of his wife's housekeeping services on a regular basis. In the defense of old husbands, many of these long-distance marital relationships are placed under considerable pressure. Only male-female relationships where both partners do not require constant companionship from the other (and where there is little need to monitor each other's free time) can survive prolonged long-distance commuting.

The Traveling Career Woman

My advice to a traveling career woman who intends to marry is to find a new or totally liberated husband. Other kinds of husbands will suspect you of doing the same things many of them do on business trips—scurrying around for companionship with members of the other sex. Few traditional husbands are able to gracefully accept the notion that business travel by oneself is not the exclusive province of males. One woman lamented to me about the difficulties she was having with her husband accepting her traveling in connection with her job as an admissions counselor at a college:

"Gordon knew I traveled in my job before we were married, and only complained lightly then. Now that we are married, he doesn't want me to continue my commuting trips. The worst scene came up when my boss and I (Ed) were scheduled to attend a convention together. Gordon fumed and fussed about the upcoming trip. I offered to have him accompany me, but he felt that would look like he didn't trust me and was butting into my fun. We went round and round on this one until an ironic incident happened. My boss, Ed, asked me into his office to discuss a sensitive issue.

"Ed's wife had the same uncomfortable feeling as did Gordon. She didn't want Ed to go on a business trip with me. When I told Ed about Gordie's reservations about the trip we both had a big laugh. We chalked it up to the old morality. When the dust finally settled from this colossus of prudery, all four of us went to the convention together: Me, Ed, Gordie, and his wife."

"No big issue," is the statement that best describes a new husband's attitudes toward his wife's business and professional travel. New husbands recognize that periodic travel is an exhilarating experience that benefits a male as well as a female. As one new husband candidly commented, "Now that Vera travels about once or twice a week in her job, she has come to recognize firsthand what any experienced traveler knows. Occasional travel gives you a new perspective and thus helps to prevent a work rut. But its biggest benefit is that it helps you appreciate the value of a warm, supportive home. My opinion is that even a lukewarm home beats sloshing down martinis in a crowded airport."

chapter 8

The Working Househusband

Sheldon Schachter, an easygoing full-time homemaker, climbs back into his waterbed when his wife goes off to work and his son, four-year-old Jason, to nursery school. Schachter quit his job as a psychiatric social worker to join the ranks of American househusbands. The family now gets along on one-third its former income in their four-bedroom Carmel, California, home. Mrs. Schachter finds ample job satisfaction in her part-time job teaching English to foreigners. From her point of view, it's a much better life than managing the home.

Sheldon is able to take care of the daily straightening up around the house in thirty minutes, while a full-scale housecleaning consumes only five hours once every two weeks. Enamored with the creative aspects to cooking, he is working on a book, *The Househusband's Cookbook,* which he hopes will be a successful book someday. His househusbandry has meant sacrificing restaurant meals and steaks at home, but Schachter reasons that the freedom he enjoys from not working is worth the sacrifice.

As described to a U.P.I. reporter his philosophy of work is, "I don't think anybody should work a 40 hour week. It's too draining. It's too destructive for the family. Most men can't wait to retire, when they can do the things they want. I'm doing what I want now. I'm being me. I think more men should be househusbands."[1]

Sheldon has slightly more extreme attitudes than the approximately 200,000 male homemakers in the United States recorded by the Department of Labor in 1975. However, one aspect of his life is very much in common with that of most househusbands. In addition to his housekeeping and child-tending chores, he is working at some other occupation that currently pays money, or at least holds out the promise of future money. Upon close scrutiny, most househusbands are revealed to be new or liberated husbands who are essentially underemployed, free-lance, creative types of people: artists, writers, architects, or musicians to mention a few. Added to these numbers are those of males forced into full-time homemaking on the basis of a physical or emotional disability. No examination of the new husband would be complete without a peek into the life styles of the working househusband.

Diary of a Househusband

John Morris, who has a Ph.D. in philosophy from Michigan State University, now works in the avant-garde field of computer-based artificial intelligence. His life history includes a stint as a househusband. Dr. Morris found himself between positions owing to a political rift in the college where he was employed. A staunch supporter of women's and men's liberation, his diary is both illuminating and compelling. Portraying unquestionably that not all males are well suited to the life of a househusband, John's diary is presented almost verbatim:

During the 1950s it was a popular piece of radical chicanery to paint your face black, and then pretend to want to buy a house in a white neighborhood. You got some sense, you thought, of what it might be like to be black in America. Or, you might adopt a Jewish name, and send applications to exclusive summer resorts just to see what discrimination was really like.

Since that time, of course, these masquerades have lost their charm. The radicals have adopted anti-Semitism as part of their creed, and the problems of growing up black in America have been seen to be traumatic with an intensity that a few days in blackface cannot capture.

While these games are no longer appealing, I do want to recommend a somewhat similar piece of role-playing for those men that want to learn how the better half lives. Pretend to be a housewife. Try it out for a few days; you won't be able to stand it for longer. The experiment will help give a hint of what liberation is about.

I must admit that my disguise was largely inadvertent. I lost my job while my wife was able to hang on to hers, and a year and a half of searching has not produced a new job for me. The demand for seventeenth-century metaphysicians, even very good ones, is somewhat less than overwhelming.

I taught my last class in May, gave my Mr. Chips speech to the last tearful student, and settled down to playing the role of full-time housewife. Or househusband, I suppose. My diary excerpts that follow tell the rest of the story. The selection is comparatively brief because the life of the housewife is deadly dull. Boredom, the loss of a sense of professional identity, loneliness, and the feeling that you're going absolutely nowhere—these are only the beginning of the story.

I know that some contented housewives will complain that I'm overdramatizing, but I rather wonder whether they may not be under-dramatizing their own lives. Perhaps by this time they've simply gotten used to a life in which the demands are low, the rewards are low, and there is no focus or meaning outside the home, no real people other than the spouse and children.

Monday. The phone just rang, for the first time today. Female saleswoman-type voice asked to speak to the "lady of the house." Phyllis (John's wife) was busy, so I asked, "May I tell her who's calling?" There was no reply, she hung up in my ear.

Typed out the title page for the paper I'm supposed to deliver in Minnesota next month. They want to include my "institutional identification"—the college I'm working for. I don't have any. Is an institution a source of personal identity? Can you be a free-lance person?

Tried to study again. Noam Chomsky on generative grammars. It wasn't making sense. You get an overwhelming sense of apathy. What's the point? What is there to do with it, other than teach it to someone else, in some nonexistent future classroom? You get further and further behind, more and more trapped.

Got a quart of buttermilk at the store. Used it as a starter for another gallon of buttermilk and three or four pounds of cheese. The cheese took all afternoon to make. The cheesemaking kit, a Christmas present, shows a woman feeding some of the cheese that she's made to her husband who looks ecstatic. Why doesn't he make the cheese and feed it to her? Is the whole food preparation ritual, in which the housewife's role is feeding the hungry man in the evening, simply part of the trap? Why this mystique about food?

Tuesday. The phone rang. This time Phyllis was out. I asked, "Have you tried at her office?" "No thank you," she said, "I'll call back later." This is a ritual which is repeated once a month. The caller is from Sears Roebuck trying to get a catalogue order. She never speaks to me; it's the woman's job to buy the bargains in the latest catalogue.

On the airlines, thanks to pressure from the liberationists, the stewardesses are now called flight attendants, to eliminate the suggestion that it's exclusively a woman's job. But nobody has suggested a new name for housewives. Maybe no male wants a job like this?

I suppose that there is some deep tribal instinct that says women should cook and men should hunt buffaloes, or whatever, but, like most deep tribal instincts, this one didn't take with us. Phyllis seemed to think that it was more important to finish her thesis than to spend two hours preparing dinner. Everyone else thought so too.

Good Housekeeping makes no pretenses. For

them cooking is a woman's job, and their cookbook always refers to the cook as "she." I wrote to them to complain about this, but they didn't reply. On the radio show just now, *Good Housekeeping's* advertisement refers to the consumer as "she." Apparently cooking and consuming are women's jobs.

Woman's Day tells us—judging by its editorial content—that women spend their days cooking and painting flowers on old coffee cans, or doing some other kind of mental hospital therapy. Aren't some women's days spent in repairing telephone lines or flying airliners?

There's a major difference between cookbooks written by women and those written by men. Craig Claiborne gives a receipe for Jaipur chicken curry that calls for sixteen ingredients, ranging from lime juice to homemade coconut milk. *Woman's Day* tells you to mix some curry powder with some condensed chicken soup, sprinkle cashew nuts on top, and you're through. Men cook for pleasure; women cook out of necessity.

9 P.M. The house is empty tonight. She's off working at her office, doing the final revision on her book. There's nobody around. I suppose that I could call up some out-of-town friends; former colleagues of mine who have left town. But can I justify spending three or four dollars of my wife's money for a call like that? What would my wife say when she saw the bill?

Wednesday. Sears Roebuck called again. Was my wife in? Would I tell her that the catalogue order was in so that she could pick it up? I had ordered the shower curtain myself and I would pick it up, but it seemed pointless to explain these things to Sears.

Another soup ad on the radio. They call numbers at random and ask the person to sing their commercial for them. They never call men. Men aren't supposed to be at home during the day. If they call me, I'll sing obscene songs for them.

8 P.M. Phyllis and I went to Montgomery Ward to look for a new lawn mower. The salesman explained to me about the four-cycle engine, the automatic choke, the aerodynamic design of the blades. Then he turned to Phyllis and asked, "How do you like the color?"

Thursday. The women across the street are together for their afternoon coffee klatch, with their children and dogs in the front yard. While they've been klatching for the past six months, I've finished one book and the outline for another. Maybe this is just my way of painting flowers on old coffee cans.

A woman came by just now, passing out handbills for her husband, who is running for the board of education. I have not yet heard of any men coming by passing out handbills for their wives but I guess that it must happen sometimes.

I used to have a hangup about sex roles, but it disappeared long ago. Tim Leary, who was then the straight psychological consultant for our school in Berkeley, explained my funny scores on a popular standardized personality test called the MMPI. You get a high feminine score if you want to go to a concert instead of a football game, or if you want to write poetry

> and forget about the sex roles. It was nice to be declared sane by Tim Leary.
>
> *Friday.* 3 P.M. Helped a neighbor rescue baby robin from two cats. Rescue was probably temporary. This was the first time I'd spoken to any human being since Phyllis left for her office this morning.
>
> Mail included two invitations to me as "an emancipated, thinking woman" to subscribe to *Intellectual Digest* magazine. Possibly they're using an old mailing list from the Cook Book Guild, to which I once belonged. Are cookbook buyers likely to be emancipated, thinking women?
>
> The phone hasn't rung for hours. Even a salesman would be a relief. Even Sears Roebuck.

Joe Errera, Night Watchman

A permanent or long-term physical disability is sometimes the life event that converts a full-time worker into a househusband. Once such a man becomes partially rehabilitated, he often looks for part-time employment and yet still retains his working househusband status. Such is the case of Joe Errera, described in depth by Liz Roman Gallese in the *Wall Street Journal,* March 16, 1973:

> It was a clear August night nearly 18 years ago. In a Delaware & Hudson Railroad Company train yard on the outskirts of this Hudson River mill town, trainmen were putting cars into a freight house for unloading.
>
> Joe Errera, a husky 38-year-old brakeman, stood on the front end of one boxcar, testing its brake. Finding the brake satisfactory, he let the car roll down the track and prepared to tighten

the brake and stop the car as soon as it met the car ahead. But something went wrong. "I kept tightening it . . . the car never stopped," Joe says.

The car smashed into the one ahead, and Joe was hurled onto the ground. His back was severely sprained.

The injury changed Joe's life. He was never able to do strenuous work again. But he carved out a whole new career for himself—at home, doing the cooking and cleaning, and caring for his two-year-old son, Joey. His wife, Josephine, a ninth-grade algebra teacher, became the chief breadwinner, and Joe became a homemaker.

The arrangement has continued through most of the years since the accident, even during a five-year period when Joe worked nights as a watchman to earn a little extra money but continued cooking and cleaning during the day. It hasn't always been easy. Joe became a male homemaker long before the era of women's liberation, and he had to endure more than a few raised eyebrows and subtle barbs over the years from friends and relatives who thought he should get a "real" job. . . . 18 years ago, role reversal was hardly an alternative at all, especially for somebody who fit the traditional male breadwinner role as well as Joe Errera did. Gene Gilchrist, his boss on the railroad, recalls him as a highly responsible and enthusiastic worker. "I wished I had 15 like him. Whenever I'd call—at night, on weekends, on holidays—Joe would say, 'I'll be there.'"

The son of a house painter, Joe had long been accustomed to hard work. At the age of 10, shortly after his mother died, he found his first job—hawking newspapers. After grammar school and a year of vocational high school, he signed up with the Civilian Conservation Corps and went off to camp in Oregon—because it was farthest away, he says, to help put a road through the wilderness.

Later he delivered telegrams for Western Union, pulled up gooseberry roots as part of a New Deal cleanup project, worked on an assembly line in a toothbrush factory, peddled vegetables and worked as a laborer in a military arsenal.

But Joe says he adapted easily to the role of a homemaker. Personal qualities that had long lain dormant gradually began to surface. Gentleness, for example. (When Lady, the family's puppy, would cry at night, Joe would get up and rock her to sleep.) And meticulousness. (He carefully assembled all of his wife's family recipes into a handwritten notebook titled "Josie's Recipes.")

Three years after the accident, with the help of money from an insurance settlement, the Erreras bought a white frame Cape Cod house with a garage and a spacious lawn, set in a pleasant tree-lined neighborhood of Troy. The house became Joe's workshop.

He would arise in the morning, don a baggy sweater and slacks, fix breakfast for the family, then kiss his wife and son good-bye as he left for school. He did the family marketing, fixed lunch for Joey when the youngster came home at midday, then prepared dinner.

Every morning, Joe says, he gathered the

family laundry into a bundle and put it into the washer. Then he made beds, dusted and vacuumed. He washed the kitchen floor, cleaned windows and scrubbed the bathroom.

In the summertime, Joe mowed the lawn, trimmed shrubbery and planted rows of tomatoes, lettuce, watermelons and cucumbers. On hot afternoons, he often wandered through the fields behind his house picking huckleberries for homemade pies.

Perhaps the greatest advantage of being a homemaker, Joe now says, was the opportunity to care for his son. "Joey gave me so much pleasure," he says. "I wouldn't have missed a minute of it."

"He raised Joey, really," says Josephine. "When Joey was a baby, he'd bathe him, change his diapers and care for him when he was sick. I wouldn't have known what to do."

While his son was growing up, Joe drove him wherever he had to go: school, day camp, sporting events. He coached Joey's Little League baseball team and taught him how to fish, swim, play ball and ride a bike. A playmate of Joey's recalls: "We were like three little kids playing together."

Josephine has a large, clannish family, and having Joe around proved to be a boon for it, too. Bring down food for an invalid father's dinner? Sure, Joe would do it. Meet a brother's plane? Joe would go. Send packages of food and clothing to relatives abroad? Joe would volunteer.

Joe was handy with tools, and he launched various projects around the house. In 1962, the year of the Cuban missile crisis, he built a two-room bomb shelter in his basement. "Joe was adamant about that shelter," recalls a brother-in-law. "He was always looking for ways to protect his family."

Though skilled in his role as homemaker, Joe faced a problem unique even to the most frustrated housewife: ridicule. . . . Joe says nobody has ever criticized him to his face, but he says he senses subtle ridicule from time to time. "But I don't care about it," he says. "I know what I am, and my wife knows, and she is happy. It's nobody's business."

Avoiding Explanations. Josephine admits, however, she is hurt by criticism. "At times many in my family felt he was a slacker," she says. "One would drop little innuendoes, like 'You know, Josie, some people think Joe is lazy. . . .'"

Indeed, one sister-in-law expresses her opinion this way: "He's a good man, but I guess I can't see the arrangement. How many times did he go fishing when she worked her summers out? Of course, Joey has pleasant memories of his father. But the price had to be paid, and she paid it."

Another relative says he can accept the situation only because of Joe's injury. "That wouldn't have been my role in life, but if I were disabled, I'd work in the house to pull my slack," he says. "I wouldn't approve in any other case. A man's job is working, not playing house."

Partly to avoid unnecessary explanations, Josephine says, she has avoided most social activities at school. "There are always those people who would look down on him," she says.

Everything at Home. Instead, the Erreras have centered their social activities on their home. They like nothing better than to invite relatives to lavish six-course dinners, often crowned with three homemade desserts. They watch TV or sunbathe in their backyard. "We would rather stay home," says Josephine. "We have everything we want here."

Clearly, the Erreras think their arrangement has been successful, and they think they know why. First of all, they say, Josephine has never thrown up to her husband the fact that she is the breadwinner. She makes a list of items to be bought and bills to be paid, and hands over her check to Joe. He alone handles the transactions. "I don't even want to see the money," she says.

The couple has never had financial problems. "We've never denied ourselves. We eat what we want. Our home is paid for. We have a good car and enough money to send Joey through college," says Josephine. . . .

Moreover, Josephine genuinely wants to work. She had already gone back to teaching the year before Joe's accident. The couple had been temporarily caring for Joey in shifts at that time, and had been looking for a permanent babysitter. Their family physician Dr. Nicholas F. Brignola, says, "Josephine didn't want to become trapped into being a complete home woman. After all, why should she throw away 20 years of education?"

"I longed to go back," Josephine says. "When Joey was born, I thought I'd never go back. But when September rolled around, I'd sit in the bay window and watch the kids with their knee socks and plaid bookbags. I loved teaching." *No Way to Measure.* As for Joe's role, she says, "It didn't bother me that he was doing woman's work, that's what I was supposed to be doing. He held his own and contributed to the home. I couldn't measure in money what he's given us."

It's hard, of course, to measure a homemaker's contribution. But one criterion has always been how well the offsprings develop into mature, happy adults. In Joe's case, his son has been something of an all-American boy. As a youngster, Joey played hockey and pitched for the Little League. In high school, he maintained an "A" average, played varsity soccer and was elected president of his senior class. Today he's a sophomore at Rensselaer Polytechnic Institute in Troy, preparing for medical school.

Like many other homemakers, Joe a few years ago took a stab at stepping out of the home. He got a job as a night watchman, reasoning that the work wasn't strenuous enough to aggravate his back, and with Joey nearing college age, the extra income would be handy.

The move surprised his family. He still cooked and did the major cleaning chores, but Josephine missed him so much that he would have to call her several times each night from work. Joey found that all the things he and his father used to do together had to be crammed into a Sunday afternoon.

"If it was up to me, I would have told him not to take the job," says Josephine. "We were making out. Besides, he had had a hard life. It was his turn to have something done for him."

Learning to Cope. Then Joe discovered he had a heart condition. One afternoon in the summer of 1971, while mowing the lawn, he felt faint. His doctor prescribed pills. A few days later, he became ill again and drove to a hospital.

With Joey away at college (he was then at school further from home), Josephine was left alone to drive home and fetch Joe's toothbrush and pajamas. But she hadn't driven in 20 years. Where were the car lights? she wondered. Where was the ignition keyhole? Joe had to explain. "I don't know how I made it home," she says. "Those roads . . . I was swerving all over."

She soon realized how dependent she was on Joe in other ways. The family marketing, for example. Joe had always done it. Now, what to buy? "He had her so dependent on him, she didn't even know what cuts of meat to pick up at the supermarket," says one of her sisters.

Joe, now 55, has since quit his job and continues to recuperate at home. He is deeply religious, and spends much of his time in religious study. On doctor's orders, he says he'll never return to work. He has tried to resume some of his homemaking chores, but finds them something of a burden. "I really enjoyed doing those things," he says, "I've tried to get meals going even now. But it's better if I don't. I never know when this condition will start up again. And if I feel bad, my wife feels bad."

Looking back, the Erreras say they haven't any regrets. "I don't think I would have changed anything," says Josephine. "He gave my son a wonderful upbringing. And I love it when he's home."

"Things always happen for the best, I believe," says Joe, musing on his railroad accident. "It brought me closer to my wife and son. And it proved that my wife really cared."

Indeed, says Dr. Brignola, the family physician: "Joe soaked up all the goodies of life."

The Seasonal Househusband

Yet another variety of the working househusband is the man who takes over housekeeping and child-rearing responsibilities on a full-time basis during those times in which he does not practice his usual occupation. A seasonal househusband can also be counted upon to do his fair share of domestic chores during his busy work seasons. Reverend Richard Gilbert is precisely that type of individual, as described by Mary Rita Kurycki, writing for the Rochester, New York, *Democrat & Chronicle:*

> When he was a Senior at Canandaigua Academy, playing football on Saturdays and preaching on Sundays, a newspaper reporter wrote about him: "he passes, punts, and prays."
>
> Today, at 37, the Reverend Richard Gilbert still prays, watches football on television, plays football with the neighborhood kids, serves on the Euthanasia Council, is pastor of the First Unitarian Church, is chairman of the judicial process commission of Genesee Ecumenical Ministries and is involved in a wide variety of social action movements.
>
> He's obviously a busy man. But he's also a busy father and husband who spends his freer summer months as a househusband and all year

works at being a good husband deeply involved in role-sharing with his wife.

His wife, Joyce, a project coordinator with the Public Affairs Department of Channel 21, leads a busy life too. She sings in choir, has worked with the Democratic Party, and misses the time she once had to devote to things like FISH (Friends in Service Here).

Together they are raising two young boys, Matthew, 7, and Douglas, 5. They're finding the time in their busy days to do little things like meeting in Avon to shop for a new couch or spending two hours most evenings playing with the children.

The lifestyle they've chosen hasn't been easy, but they'd not have it any other way. It's not something they thought out or discussed before they got married 13 years ago. It just sort of happened because they are the people they are.

Their house isn't the neatest, the most immaculate, they admitted. "What little is done is done by both of us," Joyce Gilbert said. "If something needs doing, the one it bothers the most does it. Neither of us LIKES housework."

He mows the lawn—"because I'm ecologically minded and still use the old-fashioned rotary hand mower. It would take her 16 times as long to do it." She does the cooking, "because I'm no good at it," Rev. Gilbert said.

But he packs lunches for all in the morning, "because I usually have more time." She handles finances, bill paying, check-writing, "because she likes to and is good at it."

"But we don't comment on each other's expenditures. We talk over major expenditures like car, house. But if he wants to send a donation to a favorite cause, that's his decision," she said.

Together they are raising their children and when any decision concerning the children must be made, they discuss the problem in front of the children "so they can see we're jointly participating in the decision," he said.

Their lifestyle has worked out so that it's Mr. Gilbert and not Mrs. who volunteers along with other mothers to drive nursery school children to the Planetarium for a day.

Though it's often hard to find the spare time, Gilbert makes time to play with his own kids and neighbors' children. He's proud to tell of the time a little kid came to the back door and wanted to know "Can Mr. Gilbert come out and play?"

They entered their marriage as "two independent professionals," they said. She was a teacher, he a minister. They continued as such until their first child was born. Then she took off several years from work "for the purely selfish reason I wanted to be home with them during their early years." It's only been a little more than a year since she's been back at work.

"I'm no house frau, as you could see if you dropped by our house. I work because I prefer to be doing something. I didn't go to college (and earn a graduate degree in radio, television and film) and work seven years to throw it all away," she said.

So last summer, Rev. Gilbert found himself with much more free time than his wife and two little boys who needed supervision. He became a househusband.

"I found that I had no extra time, even though both boys were in camp. By the time I got one dropped off it was time to go get the other, or put one to bed for a nap or stop at the store for something. I really developed an empathy for those women who are in traditional housewife roles. You're limited because so much necessary tasks must be accomplished."

But it wasn't as difficult for Rev. Gilbert to be a househusband as it might be for many men, his wife added.

"Right from the beginning when Matthew was born he wanted to do everything except breastfeeding."

"Every man should be required to be self-sufficient, to be able to function on his own and raise his children. We're very proud to be interchangeable parts—each can earn a living, each can take care of home and kids. Of course, we have varying talents for those things," he said.[3]

How Neighbors and Visitors React

Househusbands—particularly the working kind—are receiving increasing acceptance at the intellectual but not necessarily at the emotional level. On the basis of about ten articles in women's magazines and numerous newspaper articles, the idea of the male who stays at home no longer shocks most people. But at the grass roots, neighborhood level—particularly in suburbia—a working or nonworking househusband is still an item of curiosity and disbelief. Many suburbanites, or visitors to suburbia, may have read about househusbands, but the basic concept isn't something they are able or willing to accept when they encounter a househusband face to face.

A reasonable analogy is that of people's reactions to an attractive call girl as a neighbor. Most people have read about high-priced call girls living in the midst of affluent people engaged in the most conventional occupations. The idea of having a $200 per night neighbor sounds almost titillating. But, when a neighbor is actually suspected of prostitution, most people want her to hurriedly relocate. There is a basic split between people's attitude and their behavior. On paper, they are tolerant. In practice they are not.

Brent, a friend of mine, works as a free-lance architect. Rather than incur the expense of a formal office, he works out of his home. Much of his work is done on a subcontract basis for several other firms who require his services only during periods of peak business activity. Brent estimates that by working at home, his effective income is about $6,000 higher than if he rented an office. His figures include items such as office rent, auto expenses, lunches, additional clothing, and the tax advantages of an office at home. He operates from a town-house apartment in suburban Buffalo, while his wife, Hillary, goes to her office as a school social worker. Brent and his wife have no children, but they do have a large boxer dog. Brent shares with us some of his experiences as a working househusband.

> Of all the ridiculous experiences I've had as a work-at-home male, the Welcome Wagon lady tops the list. Two weeks after Hillary and I moved into the complex, I received an 11 A.M. visit from the local Welcome Wagon representative. She seemed perplexed when I answered the door. I explained matter of factly that my wife

was not home but that, since Hillary and I share homemaking, I would happily listen to her presentation. Gingerly she stepped inside the door, looking over her shoulder as if to determine if anyone else in the neighborhood saw her entering my townhouse. I offered her coffee but she mumbled a polite "No thank you."

It was an unusually sunny April day for Buffalo, making our kitchen quite warm. I extended an offer to hang up Miss Welcome Wagon's coat. She jumped back as if we were just introduced at a cocktail party and I had tried to put my hand in her pants. She then sat on the edge of the kitchen chair with her coat tightly closed, racing through her presentation of gift rain bonnets, car washes, book markers, and discounts on furniture and clothing. She only paused to remind me not to forget to tell Mrs. __________ about these valuable coupons.

Perhaps just to tease her a bit, I gestured that I would like to shake hands good-bye. Upon her leaving again she stiffened up. As she left, she peeked to see if anybody might be observing her leaving.

The head maintenance man is kind of a friend of mine. I see him frequently when I step outside the apartment for a quick jog or simply to rest my eyes from the heavy concentration required in my work. When we do chat for a minute or so, I usually ask him questions or make comments that I assume are relevant to him, such as commenting about how well kept the grounds are.

Maybe, the clothing I wear around the neighborhood would suggest that I'm either unemployed or marginally employed. Whatever it is, my maintenance man friend had formed his own analysis of my occupational status. One day he came over late in the afternoon to fix a leaking faucet. He commented, "I would have come over earlier, but I figured you would be sleeping. I take it you work nights at the Chevy plant a few miles from here." When I told him I was an architect, he replied, "When does your unemployment insurance run out?" People somehow just can't comprehend the idea that a man can be productively employed and yet work at his house.

I'm not a wealthy architect, but it would seem to me that I make about twice as much money as the average tenant at Williamsville Manor. Yet, because I stay home and am seen toting groceries and sweeping the porch, people think I am to be pitied. Even worse, a few of the neighbors I encounter make subtle, derisive comments to me. A woman who lives a few town houses away and I happened to arrive at the mailbox simultaneously. This was the first time we chatted.

With a sarcastic smirk, she said to me, "Pretty nice hours you have." I told her I worked the normal working hours. Then she said, "Oh, when does your wife get her chance to go on vacation?" I replied, "Not until she saves enough money to buy us a house in the country." We haven't exchanged pleasantries since.

Neighborhood children are really the most accepting of a work-at-home male like myself. They have to depend upon me in emergencies. Late one fall afternoon a neighborhood child rang my bell about ten times in one minute. I figured an accident had happened, but fortunately I was wrong. They were just trying to settle a dispute over what happens when somebody gets tackled in his end zone in a football game. Another time they requested my services to help extricate a box kite from a tree.

My overall reaction to being a househusband (and I'm not sure I like that term) is that it's a sensible way of life. Working at home is one of the most practical answers to the problem of congested highways and the energy crisis. A lot of traditional people cannot fathom the fact that a male can stay at home, and yet still be ambitious and productive. It's their problem, not mine.

chapter 9

Sex and the New Husband

Sex is another area in which many new husbands distinguish themselves. However, all new husbands are not alike in their sexual proclivities, preferences, and attitudes. New husbands can be found who ambitiously pursue extramarital liaisons, while many others are relatively monogamous in their life styles. A minuscule number of new husbands are bisexual, while the vast majority are heterosexual. New husbands, subject to the stresses of everyday living often faced by other males in society, are sometimes impotent. New husbands can be found who swing with intensity, although most tend to perceive swinging as a symptom of failure in their marriages. Occasionally a new husband finds himself in a relationship whereby his wife is unable to achieve orgasm, yet most report good sexual satisfaction on the part of their wives.

New husbands sometimes have the need to conjure up images of an attractive neighbor or movie star while having sexual intercourse with their wives; yet most find the visual stimulation of their wives sufficiently interesting to focus on reality during sex. A new husband might be found who sees sex as an isolated part of living, but most new husbands regard sex with their wives as one vital aspect of the total male-female communication process.

What the sex life of the new husband tends to be, and *not to be,* and how he differs in attitude from other men is an illuminating topic. It helps to explain why the new husband is often having the most fun out of sex, even though he may be receiving the least amount of publicity. In the sexual realm, new husbands have much more in common with liberated husbands than they do with old husbands. This chapter will help explain why.

The Supermasculine Ego

To many an old husband, power and control are associated with masculinity. In order to perform well sexually (frequency of intercourse, stiffness of erection, and perhaps pleasing his partner), some men need to feel that they wield the biggest amount of power in most aspects of the marital relationship. A man who fundamentally equates masculinity with power often feels unmasculine when he shares decision making about important matters with his wife (or girlfriend). Feeling unmasculine, his sexual performance is likely to be adversely affected. Household power is equated (perhaps unconsciously) with sexual power and performance.

A number of old husbands have told me that, if they shared household tasks with their wives, they would lose the feeling of being the dominant partner in the relationship. Fear is expressed by these men that the loss of dominance in everyday living would mean that they would no longer be dominant sexually. According to their view of the world, loss of male dominance in bed (or wherever else sex is practiced) leads to sexual failure.

Cedric, an old husband from New Zealand, expresses the typical concern some men have about the relationship between egalitarian relationships and sex: "I think that if a man and his wife shared equally in decision making and household chores, it would have a distinct effect upon their sex life. A normal man would feel that he is not in a commanding position which is important to many men. Thus, he would often feel impotent and question his identity. Men like to feel that they are the dominant force, even if it is not to a great degree, but within reason. To my knowledge, most women prefer this type of man too.

"Two people cannot be the aggressor in sex. It is the mark of a passive man who begins to allow a woman to take over his responsibilities in life. When he does this and also allows the woman to take the initiative in sex, he is sacrificing some of his masculinity. Bad sex is often the result."

Sharing Improves Sex

Cedric, the man from down under just quoted, may be right for a person of his values and beliefs. But, for an increasing number of males who have become new husbands (or have always been), the sharing pattern has led to improvements in their sex lives. Sharing decision making, household tasks, and child rearing with their spouses tends to reduce a myriad of small tensions and potential feelings of resentment that often occur when these aspects of living are not shared. In situations where one spouse wants to be dominated (the old-fashioned wife or the henpecked husband), sharing could lead to decreased sexual enjoyment. Frustrations stemming from the basic nature of a marital relationship are often the force underlying most sexual problems in a relationship. For the moment we are concerned with the pleasant sexual byproducts derived from the sharing pattern when the wife and husband *want* sharing.

Byron H. Knight, an education strategist from Atlanta, enjoys a sharing relationship with his wife. Aside from spending about ten hours a week helping in the rearing of his three-year-old child, he devotes about five hours a week to cooking, cleaning, laundering, and gardening. His wife works as a secretary. Byron makes this comment about the effects of sharing on a couple's sex life together:

"I think it enriches sex life. It places a more equal emphasis on the partnership aspect of sex as opposed to one dominant and one submissive person, so frequently learned as the roles one is 'supposed to play.'"

Thayer L. Parrish, a securities representative and insurance agent, offers a complex psychological explanation of how sharing improves sex that speaks for many new husbands: "I believe everyday mundane roles affect sex-role situations. In many cases the more dominant person (the one making most of the everyday decisions) must also be called upon to make sexual decisions or be the aggressor, ultimately causing repression of normal feelings in the other person and finally causing problems in the relationship. I think if decisions are shared and if we assume it can carry over to the sexual side of the relationship, then a more healthy sexual role identification could result. No one likes to be the initiator all the time."

Roy, a cost accountant and converted new husband, represents a telling case history of how changing a marital pattern from completely separate roles to one of sharing had a profound influence upon this couple's sex life:

"My wife and I used to do everything that you're not supposed to do according to a book like *Open Marriage*. I was the breadwinner while she stayed home and took care of the children. I took care of the household books, she did all the cooking, and too much of the child rearing. Perhaps I was the most at fault for that arrangement, but we were both products of the life styles we learned from our parents. A couple of magazine articles helped us realize that we were doing things wrong in our relationship.

"Once our last child was in school we began to change our marriage around. Marie took a job. We discussed things more and began to divide up the chores of daily living. We started questioning little rituals like my making the cocktails before dinner while Marie made the hors d'oeuvres or served the nuts. I began clearing the table. Marie would sometimes clean the garage. But, more important than that, we began to share our thoughts and fears about almost everything. Sure, some of our close discussions seemed to do more harm than good. For instance, Marie's feelings were hurt for a week when I told her once that perhaps if we had both married at later ages we might have made different choices in partners. But the net effect of our new closeness was good. Particularly in sex.

"I have an expression I use to describe what sex is like with Marie when she's unhappy about something. I call it 'sulky sex.' In the past we had many evenings where Marie said 'Yes' with her mouth but 'No' with her body. She just kind of sulked and went through the motions of sex. Now we make an attempt to talk out our problems before they lead to sulking. Then when we do have sex, Marie's with it in both body and spirit.

"I'm not trying to paint the picture of my wife as the villain and me as the complete hero. Quite often I would be brooding over a problem and because of it do a damn perfunctory job of sex. Marie claims that since we began our plan of sharing problems I wait until I have at least rolled off her before going to sleep. In the past I sometimes fell asleep right on top of her.

"We are both emotionally looser in sex, and that has helped us enjoy sex much more. Up until a couple of years ago, Marie never had more than one orgasm in a session of lovemaking. Now it's not unusual for her to come two or three times. She claims her change in sexual enjoyment stems from her feeling closer to me. I think too that now we get along better I'm more relaxed and can stay with sex longer.

"After several hours of discussion on the topic, Marie and I are both convinced that she no longer uses sex as a bartering device. I guess a lot of women have grown up believing that sex is something you give your husband as a reward for something nice he's done for you. If I agreed to take Marie some place she wanted on vacation, it would improve our sex for a few days. The same thing would happen if I gave her an extra nice Christmas present. She would be more sexually responsive that night.

"There would also be a negative aspect to this sexual bartering. If I wasn't nice to Marie—in whatever nice meant at the time—she would hold back a little on sex. I remember once we had an argument over whether or not we needed an automatic dishwasher. I felt we didn't and she felt we did. Marie was as enthusiastic as a sack of wheat in bed until I finally agreed to buy a dishwasher."

Sexual Problems

An encouraging medical development was recently described in the *Los Angeles Times*. According to the report, "A plastic device that solves the physical problem of impotence due to injury or certain diseases has been implanted in more than 300 male patients by a University of California at Los Angeles urologist."[1] Dr. Robert O. Pearman said he developed the penile prosthesis because "Nobody in the medical profession was doing anything to help these unfortunate people." This urologist helps these disease or accident victims by surgically implanting a silicone shaft in the penis which serves as a so-called scaffold, enabling normal sexual intercourse.

Even if this device were perfected, only about 10 to 15 percent of the impotent males could be helped. The remaining 85 to 90 percent of the cases of impotence stem from psychological factors, making such cases untreatable by Dr. Pearman's method. Nonphysical causes of impotence are extremely difficult to isolate with certainty. Usually a good deal of speculation is required to specify what particular problem or pressure underlies a given case of male impotence. Perhaps 100 different causes of impotence have been postulated by a variety of sex experts.

A startling observation about these postulated causes of impotence is that they relate to problems that are more characteristic of old than new husbands, of nonsharing than sharing relationships. Advances in sex therapy that have shown promising results intentionally focus on improving the relationship between a male and female. Often the relationship is helped to move in the direction of the type of relationship characteristically experienced by a new (or totally liberated) husband and his wife.

Admittedly, an improvement in the relationship begins on a somewhat mechanical basis. Both partners are encouraged to touch and fondle each other in a gentle, caring manner. Acting in a gentle, caring manner in turn leads to feeling that way. A segment of the diary of a woman describing her experiences at the famous Masters and Johnson sex clinic, illustrates this process:

"It was a beautiful experience for both of us. The doctors had recommended that Tim spread a silky soft lotion all over my body. He had really learned his lesson about touching me gently and kissing me. He blew in my ear as he spread the lotion on my neck and back. He ran his tongue across my toes as he touched the inside of my thigh. All the while his face was one of a man who loved his wife and wanted to satisfy her. I could see our life together improving, right in that motel room. We knew we were on the way to working out our problems."

Not coincidentally, many of the factors associated with impotence in males are also associated with frigidity in females. New husbands and their wives, it appears strongly, are less prone to have these problems than are old husbands—who quite often are married to very traditional women. Irving London, M.D., has pinpointed what accounts for a substantial proportion of sexual malfunction among people with traditionally routine relationships. His observation is quoted in the book *Men and Masculinity:*

> When doing frigidity counseling work for Masters and Johnson, I was struck by a recurring story. The man of the house would come home, have a couple of drinks, eat dinner, plop down in front of the television, drift off into a semistuporous state, and be helped to bed by his wife. Revived to a half-awake condition by this activity, he finds the stamina to roll over on top of his beloved and following a few furtive swipes, plunges home for a two minute stint as he falls asleep. She, dejected, depressed, frustrated and guilt ridden, lies in bed asking herself, "What's wrong with me? Why can't I climax?" Maybe they come for help.[2]

Medical journals and popular magazines frequently carry articles presenting a sexologist's opinion about what factors bring about impotence (or its variant, premature ejaculation) in males. As valuable as these opinions are, it is equally informative to see what husbands themselves say brings about such problems. A sampling of twelve husbands' opinions about what they think could be an important factor underlying impotence is presented next. New husbands and totally liberated husbands would seem to have fewer of these conflicts—although virtually no male has absolute immunity to impotence.

Husband A: "A wife nagging a husband could make him impotent. The constant nagging is like water dripping on your head. If she keeps it up long enough, you might not even want to raise it."

Husband B: "Competition between a husband and wife could cause such a problem. At one time my wife and I used to compete about everything, even about who was the best sex partner. Eventually, I was on edge even when we were in bed together. Once we worked out our problems, my staying power went back to normal."

Husband C: "When my wife rejected me as a person, it made good sex together almost impossible. There was just no way I could tell my sex organ to be good to a woman who was rejecting me."

Husband D: "My sex life went down the drain when our department was working sixty hours per week just to keep our heads above water. My company was trying to get double production out of every manager in the plant. What they didn't realize is that they were also playing havoc with our personal lives. When you're in the midst of a job crisis you tend to forget about sex. I won't make that mistake again."

Husband E: "I'm no sex expert, but I can tell you from common sense that the number one cause of impotence in America is when a woman belittles the manhood of her husband. Most of us shouldn't have such problems but we do. Just tell a man that he's not earning as much money as a man should and it's like telling him his penis is too small to arouse a woman."

Husband F: "The fear that I won't do well in bed is enough to make me perform poorly. I guess sex isn't something you should worry about, but it isn't easy to convince yourself that you shouldn't worry. It's a little bit like standing on a putting green and worrying that you won't be able to hit the ball in a straight line. Sure enough you won't be able to if you worry about it."

Husband G: "It's that Goddamned pursuit of success that causes impotence in so many men. If you aren't making it big in the world outside, somehow you are supposed to feel inadequate. Since a man's sexual performance is regulated much more by his brain than by his gonads, feeling inadequate can make your erection go limp in a hurry. That's if you're lucky enough to get an erection at all."

Husband H: "My first wife tried to domineer in every aspect of our relationship. That about killed things for me sexually. I grew up believing that the man is supposed to be at least equal in a relationship, if not the dominant person. I heard a couple of other men complain that a domineering woman makes it difficult for them to get it on sexually. I guess I have the same problem, at least to a mild degree. I like to think that my concern about who is the dominant partner in a relationship is beginning to disappear."

Husband I: "A man feeling unwanted or unneeded can ruin the sex life of a sensitive man. It's difficult for me to see any other justification for being married to someone unless you are wanted or needed. Without that you could shrivel up emotionally. Your penis can then shrivel up at the same time. Having sex with a woman who really doesn't need him is an almost guaranteed way to make a man impotent."

Husband J: "A sure ticket to impotence is for a wife to use sex as punishment. If a woman is angry at you and decides to get even by holding out on sex, you'll eventually get even with her by being unable to perform when she wants you. I recall a few years ago that somebody was trying to get women to stop wars on the basis of sex power. No more sex until bills are passed in Congress to end war. That might have ended wars, but it would also have created an epidemic of men with limp sex organs."

Husband K: "One thing that can cause impotence for sure is when a man wants to get rid of a woman, but he's too scared to make the break. Without his realizing what's happening, his sex performance could get worse and worse. In this situation it would be fairest to the woman and to himself to make the break."

Husband L: "As a minister and marriage counselor I can tell you that most impotence is caused by the guilt feelings men have about extramarital affairs. Whether they tell their wives or not about the affair, the guilt lingers on in the man who is a true believer in Christ. Many of the sex problems facing American men today would be eliminated if the practice of adultery were ended."

The Affair

In the minds of many people, the term *liberated husband* means a promiscuous married man—one who is free enough to have an affair whenever the thought pleases him. In the context of this book, the term *liberated* means being liberated from rigid definitions of male versus female roles. A new husband is not necessarily a sexual libertine who leads a wide-ranging polygamous sex life. The incidence of extramarital affairs among new husbands might even be *lower* than that for married men in general. What is considered average is, of course, difficult to pin down. Among college-educated males under the age of fifty, about 40 percent have had at least one extramarital affair during the course of their marriages. (Wives of these men trail them by only about six percentage points!)

If new husbands do have fewer, or briefer, affairs than do traditional husbands, it is because the types of marital relationships they have tend not to fall prey to the problems that foster affairs. Correspondingly, wives of new husbands might have less reason to look for sex and affection outside of marriage.

Old husbands often have sex outside of marriage as a tactic of counterresentment. In essence, they are seeking sex outside the marriage as a way of retaliating against the wife's resentment about what she feels is a suppressive relationship. A genuine sentiment often expressed by old husbands is "I can't understand why my wife is so unhappy about our relationship. I give her everything she wants and I take care of all the big problems that arise." What a husband of this type doesn't realize is that his wife is seeking independence, not more control. Believing that resentment is unwarranted, the old husband expresses his counterresentment by means of sex with other women.

A good deal of suppressed hostility exists in the relationships of most couples. Affairs represent a classic way of venting suppressed hostility. New husbands and their wives are not immune from mutual feelings of hostility, but they are more likely to express this hostility to each other in constructive ways. A new husband familiar to me was becoming increasingly annoyed by his wife's frequent adulatory references to tall, blond men (he was short and dark). He finally reacted with this comment:

"I'm getting ticked off at your comments about tall,

blond men. If you're tired of living with a short, dark man let me know now. If you are just looking for a way to zap me, let me know that too. I hate these indirect digs."

Confronted with this honest statement, his wife explained that her many references to blond men were really just an attempt to upset him. She had been angered by what she thought was his waning enthusiasm for her appearance. The dialogue that ensued acted as a relief valve to potential pent-up mutual hostility. A route taken by some men would have been to seek out an extramarital affair rather than confront the problem of hurt feelings directly.

Boredom of almost any variety can precipitate a sexual dalliance. New husbands, as we describe them, are more resistant to boredom than most men because of their multiple satisfactions in life. Most new husbands are getting kicks out of work and home life, thus having less need for an affair. Evidence has been collected recently that successful businessmen have many fewer affairs than do most men.

Dr. Harry J. Johnson, Chairman of the Life Extension Institute, collected anonymous questionnaires from about 6,000 Manhattan executives who visited the institute for annual physical health examinations. Included in this survey were questions about extramarital affairs. Only 21 percent reported that they had affairs, and 75 percent of these men did so only occasionally. (It does not necessarily follow that successful men in fields other than business have similar extramarital sex habits.)

As one executive commuter commented, "My work takes up so much of my energy and time that I hardly could fit a mistress into my schedule. However, if you run into an attractive woman who is willing to have an affair during a committee meeting or on a commuter train, give me her number."

Albert Ellis notes that one of the many unhealthy reasons married people have affairs is to help them cope with their sexual disturbances. Thus the married male who is impotent (or virtually so) with his wife, looks for a partner with whom he can be more potent. It would be errant nonsense to claim that no new husbands have sexual disturbances, but, for reasons discussed earlier, it is reasonable to conclude that new husbands have fewer sexual disturbances. Not having to prove himself sexually adequate, the new husband has less need for an affair than his old husband counterpart who is more prone to sexual disturbance. The wife, also, who performs adequately at home has less need for extramarital sex.

Marital escapism, Ellis also notes, is another reason many married people look outside of marriage for sex. Rather than face their marital and family problems many couples opt for extramarital liaisons. New husbands are sometimes among those to choose this route, but new husbands usually have less reason to *escape* than do old husbands. A distinguishing characteristic between old and totally liberated husbands is the fact that liberated husbands try to breathe new life into their marriages by maintaining open lines of communication between themselves and their wives. Few new husbands are boring people; therefore their marriages tend to be less boring.

When new husbands do have extramarital affairs, it would appear they often do so for *healthy* reasons. Albert Ellis hypothesizes that many normal, well-adjusted people conduct extramarital affairs discreetly without intending to do harm to their marriages. Instead of having an affair out of revenge, hostility, or to compensate for a sexual disturbance at home, the new husband might have outside sex just for fun.

Sexual varietism is one of the healthy reasons for extramarital sex postulated by Ellis. A good deal of social conditioning is required to make people—particularly males—

want to be monogamous. One man, in responding to a sex survey, reported that he had only one sexual experience with a person other than his wife in his twenty years of marriage. "Would you believe that all my life I wondered what it would be like to have intercourse with a real red-head. Well I finally found out what a real redhead looks like naked. At one time I wondered what it would be like to ride in a helicopter. One ride was enough for me there, too."

Social and cultural inducements exist for people to participate in extramarital sex in certain limited situations. When a new husband (or anybody else) engages in sex at these moments, the reasons can hardly be classified as pathological. Dr. Ellis states in his paper, "Healthy and Disturbed Reasons for Having Extramarital Relations":

> Literally millions of average Americans occasionally or frequently engage in adultery because it is the approved social thing to do at various times and in certain settings which are a regular part of their lives. Thus, normally monogamous males will think nothing of resorting to prostitutes or to easily available non-prostitutes at business parties, at men's club meetings, or at conventions. . . . This may not be the healthiest kind of adulterous behavior but it is well within the range of social normality and it often does seem to satisfy, in a socially approved way, some of the underlying sensible desires for sexual experience, adventure, and varietism that might otherwise be very difficult to fulfill in our society.[3]

And even new husbands might sometimes feel this way.

Plural Sex

A minister who regularly organizes swinging parties—group sex in which loads of people are involved—told me about a typical problem encountered in many such groups. "It's just like the newspaper accounts of mate swapping (a simple switching of partners among two couples) and swinging. It is usually the husband who initiates the idea of the couple experimenting with a swinging party. The woman is usually somewhat reluctant, but with just a little urging she agrees to try it once.

"A consistent pattern shows up. The husband enjoys the idea of playing sexually with a few different women in one evening. It's kind of the fulfillment of a life-long fantasy, even if all the women don't have first-rate figures. But then the husband gets awfully uptight when he discovers that his wife is enjoying the experience more than he is. Many men somehow want group sex for themselves, but can't accept the fact that their wives might enjoy swinging.

"Another consistent problem we have had at the groups I have organized, and at many other groups I have heard about, is that the men who come to swinging parties do not want a homosexual experience. However, the women are much more often willing to try a little homosexual escapade. It might begin with one woman patting the breasts and buttocks of another, almost as if to console her for her husband having dragged her to the party. Soon the sexual activity between the two heightens. From what I have observed, a typical swinging husband is revolted when he sees his wife engaging in oral sex with another woman.

"For reasons like this, many men are dropping out of swinging. It's another perversion of the dual-standard principle in our country."

The good reverend just quoted seems to have pointed to a very recent trend toward a growing revulsion with plural sex among its practitioners. Duane Denfield, a researcher from the University of Connecticut, has discovered that a large number of swingers have wound up disgusted and revolted from the experience. Apparently, guilt finally got to most of them, combined with the inevitable problems resulting from emotional involvement with nonspouses. Other problems included simple boredom, concern when a spouse became "too popular," or wives who "were unable to take it."

Where does the new husband fit into the plural sex (mate swapping and swinging) picture? First of all, the fragmentary evidence we have suggests that most group sexers are more likely to be old husbands or liberated husbands—not new husbands. Early reports about swingers included the fact that most of them were middle Americans—somewhat straightforward, conservative individuals with normal middle-class values. Old husbands tend to be clustered in this category.

Another picture of the swinger was drawn by sociologist Brian G. Gilmartin in his findings about suburban mate-swappers, or "recreational swingers," as he describes them. These are people who generally belong to swinging clubs with stable and limited membership, and who value the social aspects of swinging almost as they do the sexual. Swinging to them is another interesting alternative to a bowling league. Gilmartin found in his intensive study of 100 swinging couples (reported in *Psychology Today*) that most of them were very conventional people. Their incomes and educational levels were slightly lower than those of a comparison group of 100 couples in the same neighborhood, but they were less committed to church, relatives, and politics.

My own information suggests that, in addition to the

conventional types, many swingers are completely liberated people seeking total fulfillment in life. Such fulfillment often includes a pleasant orgy among good friends. But, even among the totally liberated types, swapping and swinging frequently speed along the dissolution of a relationship.

Stanley, a new husband, presents a view of plural sex that reflects the view of many other new husbands. "My wife and I have had the opportunity to get involved with group sex, but we mutually agreed to can the idea. We simply took an analytical look at the pros and cons of swinging for us, and politely said 'No' to the couple that invited us. Sure, an evening of sex with multiple partners would be a big thrill for me, but the long-range consequences might be very adverse. If I saw Bernice in bed with another man or woman, it would give me an eerie feeling. I know that Bernice would feel about the same. One evening of thrills might destroy a relationship we have been building for seven years.

"Swinging reminds me of automobile racing or ski jumping. A few moments of kicks can result in consequences that wipe out many years of developing something very important to you."

The Bisexual Mode

Leslie, a totally liberated husband, expresses his philosophy of sex in this manner. "I am a free person in the sexual sense. I don't consider myself to have one predominant sexual orientation. Sometimes I'm gay, sometimes I'm straight, but usually I'm a combination of both. No, my wife has never caught me in bed with another man, but we're open about my need for male as well as female companionship.

"Before we were married, I never pretended that I had an exclusive preference for women. I used to go off on an occasional weekend trip with a close buddy of mine.

Sometimes it was hunting, sometimes it was fishing, and once in a while just general travel. Nellie, my fiance at the time, caught on to my sexual proclivities when it was apparent that these trips left me physically exhausted. The problem was more than physical. Somehow, after a weekend of sex with a man, I just couldn't shift gears immediately into the heterosexual mode. Nellie developed an understanding of my sexual desires and accepted the situation.

"After Nellie and I became a married couple, she had no objections to my inviting one of my male friends over for dinner once in a while. I had thought of trying to get the three of us into a sexual scene, but I dropped the idea. My sex with Nellie was precious to me. So was my sex to any male friend I might have at the time. If I tried to mix the two, it might have upset a delicate balance.

"If Nellie were a more possessive person, I'm sure my life style and hers would not work out. As things stand now, Nellie and I are happy together, and I'm happy with my freedom to fully enjoy the sexual side of life."

Very few new husbands are as free (or want to be as free) as totally liberated Les. New husbands appear to be strongly heterosexual, with one important exception. Male homosexuals involved in gay marriages relate to their spouses in the same manner as do new husbands with respect to concern for feelings and sharing of household tasks. (But this book is about new husbands, not new *gay* husbands.)

An important difference between new husbands and old husbands with respect to bisexuality is that new husbands are more tolerant. Old husbands tend to denounce bisexuality as a perversion, while many new husbands look at bisexuality as simply a preference. A comment made in an all-male encounter group of middle managers from industry illustrates this tolerance.

Each member of the group was given an opportunity

to describe how he felt about every other member in the group. After the initial hour of pleasant exchanges, participants in the group became increasingly candid. Ted turned to Mike (a sensitive and physically attractive male) and said, "You know Mike, if I had any gay inclinations at all, I would make a play for you." Mike replied, "Okay Ted, whatever turns you on." The rest of the group laughed in a way that saved Ted from embarrassment.

Sexploration Together

A distinguishing characteristic of many new husbands is that they lead an exciting monogamous sex life. A new husband is able to ward off the sexual blahs by the gourmet sexual appetite he and his wife frequently share. Although new husbands rarely represent the lunatic fringe of men who derive kicks from sadistic sex, they are bold experimenters within the confines of heterosexual monogamy. New and liberated husbands, for instance, often use sexually explicit films as a way of sharpening their sex techniques or verifying whether or not they are keeping up with the state of the art. An older husband is more likely to watch sexually explicit films as a means of vicarious satisfaction. His sex life at home has often fallen into the trap of dull routine.

New husbands somehow are able to integrate sex into the mainstream of their marital relationships. Sex to them is but one more form of communicating to someone they love. Wade, an athletic and virile high school chemistry teacher (and new husband), has this view of marital sex:

"Allison and I are terrific communicators. We've only been married for three years, and yet we communicate in over a hundred little ways. I can tell by the pucker on her lips whether or not she agrees with an idea of mine. She claims she can read the width of my pupils. If I'm really excited about something my pupils enlarge. She also tells me that my pupils get real small when I'm in strong disagreement with her. I can tell by her gait when she walks in the door whether or not she had a good day with her students (she is also a teacher).

"Our sex together is another example of how well we communicate. Allison and I dance together a lot, giving us an outlet for physical communication in addition to sex. We are as smooth in bed as we are on the dance floor. But the way we go about sex is not like we are trying to compete at sexual gymnastics. I can tell by the most subtle gestures on her part where and how Allison wants to be stimulated. She can do the same with me. The first time we had sex on a chair I just glided her naturally over to the chair from the bed.

"It was as natural as leading her in a slow dance. No hesitation, no self-conscious laughing. We just were sending messages to each other with our bodies. It's the same on those occasional nights when either one of us is too tired for sex or just plain not interested in sex. No diagrams have to be drawn. No apologies. Allison's favorite statement about not wanting sex that particular night is 'Wade, I'm looking forward to our sex tomorrow night. It will have been a two-day layoff.' Communication like that doesn't give me any reason to think I'm being rejected."

What specifically is so different about the sex lives of new husbands in comparison to old husbands? A tentative answer can be inferred from the results of a *Psychology Today* sex survey. A substantial proportion of men who responded to the survey fall into the new or liberated husband categories. Among the findings supporting the contention in this book that new and liberated husbands lead rich sex lives are these interesting statistics: (1) 82 percent practice some form of oral-genital sex, strongly indicating that their sex lives are not confined to straightforward intercourse; (2) 69 percent feel very satisfied or merely satisfied with their sex lives—a figure well above the national average; (3) 73 percent claim that they are aroused by erotic or pornographic material. Assuming this is not just vicarious delight followed shortly by masturbation, it can be inferred that these husbands use erotic material in a constructive manner to fuel their sex lives.

Sexual statistics are not sufficient to fully explain the richness of the sex lives led by many new husbands who maintain exclusive relationships with their wives. More revealing is that a new husband looks upon sexual experimentation with his wife as something desirable, pleasant, and perhaps even necessary to maintain vitality in a relationship. A rigidly traditional old husband (who presumably is matched with a rigidly traditional old wife) looks outside of marriage for sexual experimentation. A sad commentary on the sex lives of many business and professional men is that they hire prostitutes for purposes of sexual experimentation. As one executive lamented, "I do all my fancy sexual relations when I'm out of town. My wife just doesn't want to know about anything but the missionary position." (Perhaps her reply would be "Try me!")

A sexual hobbyist and new husband, Paul, represents the true sexual gourmet. He told us about his sex life that is still thriving after fifteen years of marriage—with the same woman. "Bridget and I keep a file box labeled 'sex.' When either of us reads about a new sex practice or conjures up one, we make up a new file card. Since we both have access to the file, we never know who is going to try what on a given night. It's nothing mechanical, just an occasional surprise.

"One night a month, however, is 'hobby night.' On

that night we both agree to try a new variation on an old trick, or come up with something completely new. About six months ago I came upon the inspiration to pour a few drops of wine over my wife's genitals. I then proceeded to lap up the wine. She howled with delight and even had a couple of orgasms.

"Recently I tried the same trick. Again my wife howled with delight. Again she climaxed. But then she accused me of using the same trick on hobby night twice in six months. I was wrongly accused. I had switched from burgundy to chablis, but she couldn't tell the difference with the light out.

"But I'm not recommending the indiscriminate application of this wine trick, however erotic it has been for us. It's very difficult for my wife and me to order wine in a restaurant without laughing."

chapter 10

What's in It for the New Husband?

New husbands do a lot of good for their wives, children, and employers. Few women or children could rightfully object to having a caring, involved father around the house. Without a husband's help, women's liberation won't really work for a married woman. A new husband helps create a home environment that makes it possible for his wife to have a choice about the role she wants to assume in life—the true meaning of liberation. Children of a new husband enjoy the fun associated with having a loving, concerned father. Employers like to have new husbands on their payrolls because new husbands are usually involved in their work but they are not obsessed with ambition to the extent that it creates internal company problems.

Does the new husband ideology urge a man toward sacrificing his own well-being for the benefit of others? No! There are at least twelve important benefits a man might derive from being a new husband. Not every new husband is fortunate enough to receive all of these benefits. And not every new husband receives the same magnitude of pleasure from all of them. However, placed in a family situation where a wife (and children, if present) are receptive to what a new husband has to offer, *some* benefits are usually forthcoming to the new husband.

The fallout of a few personal benefits is almost inescapable in the process of making the concessions and sacrifices sometimes necessary to be a new husband. Under ideal circumstances the new husband is the beneficiary of all twelve of these beautiful by-products. Many of these benefits have already been hinted at in the preceding chapters.

Better Conversations at Home

"Sure thing," said Joel, "my wife Suzanne is a wonderful looking woman. You can imagine that I enjoy a full range of marital pleasures. Yet as I look at my marriage, it's not the sex or the status of having an attractive wife makes me so happy. It's the chance to exchange ideas and feelings with a close companion that makes my marriage to Suzanne so worthwhile.

"I did the singles scene for a long time. It was fun. I fared well in that environment, particularly because I had the financial wherewithal to hop around to the right places to meet women. But it was ghastly. Not more than one relationship a year left me with somebody I could get close to emotionally. Very few couples seem to have the potential to be tuned in to each other.

"I'll give you a prime example of what I'm talking about. I'm a scientist and inventor; naturally, I'm quite proud of my inventions. It usually takes about two years from the raw idea stage to receive the patent. I tried to explain my work to a girl I met at a resort. It was our first date. She just gave me a blank stare and then began to talk about her brother who makes candles. Her point was that her brother and I were really in the same kind of business. I had to worry about getting my ideas patented and her brother had to worry about selling his candles to storekeepers or to people on street corners.

"Maybe you're thinking that I'm egotistical because I need to tell somebody about my accomplishments. I don't think that is true. Suzanne listens to me but I also listen to her. After Suzanne and I had been dating for a few months, it dawned upon me that the most important purpose of any relationship is to have somebody to converse with. In comparison, everything else is just a fringe benefit."

Joel has pointed to the outstanding, day-by-day benefit of being a new husband (and a new father). Instead of taking turns talking, or simply exchanging directives and counterdirectives, new husbands and other members of their families have authentic conversations. Because a new husband is sensitive to what it is his wife and children are trying to express, he gets listened to in return.

Less Dependence in Daily Living

Old husbands often find themselves enmeshed in dependency traps because of the fixed-role ideology under which they live. Without their wives around to perform certain functions for them, they are helpless. Thus, they are dependent upon wives (or service personnel) for many aspects of daily living. Many old husbands become the butt of jokes or the subject of pity when their wives leave them permanently or even for a weekend. A few select retail stores have institutionalized this dependency by providing "executive shopping services." Faced with the task of making shopping decisions themselves, many old husband executives are flattered to have an attractive woman escort them through the store.

Admittedly, it is a status symbol to be personally escorted through a retail store (or to have prospective purchases brought to your office) but it is also an insult to a man's aesthetic tastes. By using a shopping escort the executive is admitting he is dependent upon a female to shop for gifts.

Dan, an old husband, was sitting outside the tennis clubhouse one July Fourth weekend. With considerable sincerity, he was complaining to those around him how his wife had ruined his weekend. When asked, "How's that?" he replied: "Maybe it's not something that you worry about, but I like to have home-cooked meals and clean tennis clothing (his tennis attire was remarkably unkempt). My wife decided that she and the children would visit her mother in Pennsylvania over this weekend. She left me with no clean tennis outfits. That means I have to either buy new outfits or wear last weekend's clothing.

"The food situation is even worse. I just hate eating out more than one meal a weekend, especially after I've come back home from a long business trip. Since my wife has gone for the weekend I have no choice but to sit in restaurants."

Dan's real tragedy is that unless his wife serves him (for example, cooks him a meal) he must hire somebody else to perform the same function. He doesn't prefer to wear rumpled tennis clothing, or to eat in lonely restaurants, but without realizing it he has become hopelessly dependent upon other people to perform simple personal services. A new husband experiences no conflict in washing out a pair of permanent press tennis shorts or preparing dinner for himself.

The hidden beauty about sharing household tasks is that a man is able to fend for himself in an emergency, or, more importantly, when he feels inclined to fend for himself.

More Fun Out of Marriage

An outstanding benefit to new (or liberated) husbands is that both marriage partners seem to have more fun out of marriage than do their more traditional counterparts. Not every nontraditional husband has a daily fiesta at home, but most generally seem to be enjoying their marriages. Few people ordinarily think of marriage as fun, but caring, sharing, and involvement at least can give a man (and his spouse) a better chance of having fun.

Scott, a new husband, expresses it this way: "You can put this down in your book about men. I've been married for a long time, and I'm having more fun than a lot of men who are newlyweds. Nanette and I have a ball together. It could be the little surprises we play on each other, or maybe the fact that neither of us has really grown up.

"Beneath it all is the way we share things. I call my wife, 'Nanette, the household transvestite,' because she's forever stealing my clothing and wearing it around the house. I had a precious custom shirt a sales manager friend of mine had given me for a birthday present. We weren't married three months when my wife claimed her right to it. Now she's taken to going out in the rain in one of my hats. In retribution, I've laid claim to her most prized wooden elephant for my den.

"Nanette and I also take turns doing the least tasteful household tasks like cleaning the bathrooms and the garbage cans. I take her out most of the time, but once in a while she takes me out or makes me a surprise dinner on a holiday. It's the surprises and the switches that keep our relationship so vibrant."

A number of years ago two sociologists concluded a

long-term study that provided additional support for the argument that the sharing type of marriage is more fun—or at least less unsatisfactory. Ernest W. Burgess and Paul Wallin interviewed approximately 1,000 couples in the late 1930s and 1940s. Four hundred of these couples were reinterviewed in the late 1950s—an undertaking unparalleled in the annals of investigations about family life. One of the most important findings of their study was that the least satisfactory were those marriages in which husbands and wives assumed the most distinct roles. Simultaneously, those marriages in which husbands and wives shared the least responsibilities were the most likely to have deteriorated into "empty shells." Sharing can indeed breathe new life into a marital relationship.

Better Sex at Home

A solution to sexual problems many married men choose is to improve upon their sex lives by seeking extramarital liaisons. This usually works until the new relationship becomes plagued with the same kind of problems that caused the first relationship to go bad. Quite often the new (and liberated) husband and his wife avoid the kinds of problems that lead to sexual dysfunction. Many of these were described in the preceding chapter. For now, we will put into clear focus how new husbands and their wives are usually able to avoid heavy doses of one emotion that is particularly disruptive to sex life—resentment. A male filled with resentment often expresses this resentment by lack of interest in sex (with his spouse) or impotence. A wife often expresses resentment by avoiding sex or performing it in a lackluster fashion.

Patriarchs have long complained about the lack of interest in sex shown by their wives. In the most rigidly traditional marriages, wives tend to look upon sexual relations as granting a favor to the husband. Part of this lack of interest in sex may well be an expression of resentment on the woman's part about having so little power in the family.

With considerable chagrin, a patriarchal executive (both in the office and at home) described a problem he and his wife were experiencing that placed them on the brink of a formal separation: "For years my wife has shown very little interest in sex. Two years ago she decided that we should sleep in separate beds. Whatever sex we did have from that point on was strictly routine. Recently we had a big blowup. Elaine somehow met one of my foremen in a neighborhood supermarket.

"Apparently they started seeing each other on a regular basis during late morning hours. He worked the night shift. Last week I came home to find Elaine under the influence of quite a few drinks. She blurted out how much she hated me for keeping her under my thumb for so many years. She told me how the foreman and she were having wild sexual encounters together; things she and I could never seem to do.

"I didn't realize up until that point that our problems had gotten so big. I figured she was just becoming frigid as she approached her mid-forties. I just don't see how we can pick up the pieces and start all over again. Half the people in the plant know about her affair with the foreman. I just couldn't keep living with my wife and face my employees. I have a certain image to maintain as a company executive."

Men, too, often accumulate resentment toward their wives. Expressions such as "the old lady" are a tip-off that many husbands resent being controlled by their spouses. New husbands are much more likely than old husbands to openly deal with such resentment when a wife attempts to domineer her husband. Henpecked men, in contrast, often take out their resentment toward their wives by a lackluster approach to sex. One man who was having sexual problems at home was asked by his sex counselor to describe the situation under which he felt the most anger toward his wife. His answer was pointed:

"She drives me up the wall when she tries to control everything I do. I don't mind her giving me advice on what clothing I should wear. I've never been very good at fashion. It's when she tries to dictate to me about areas in which I feel I should have the say. One day she told me that I should rearrange my work area in the basement; that it was too messy. Then she started to tell me that I shouldn't work more than five hours overtime per week. About a week ago she told me that it wasn't right for me to show a copy of *Playboy* to our teen-age son.

"That's when I really blew up. People call me 'mild mannered,' but I have my limits too. It was after that fight that I realized why my wife was losing some of her sexual appeal to me. I began to feel that I was going to bed with the enemy when we slept together."

Less Financial Pressure

A second income in the family is a tangible financial benefit providing two important conditions are met. For one, the wife (assuming it is the wife's income that is "second") must make enough money to cover her work-related expenses such as child care, and the additional tax burden. Second, some of the wife's income must be directed toward expenses that the husband might have incurred if the wife were not working. The woman who uses her money left over after expenses to pursue a hobby she would not have pursued if the husband had to pay for it may be having fun but she is not relieving her husband of financial burden.

Approximately 40 percent of the work force is female, and one-half of these women have live-in husbands. Thus old, new, and liberated husbands have working wives. New and liberated husbands, however, are most likely to be relieved of some financial pressures because of their wives' incomes. Poor, old husbands are not relieved of financial pressures by second incomes—they are simply staving off financial disaster. With or without a second income they remain under pressure. Old husbands at higher income levels also find little financial relief when their wives work. Men in this category are prone to consider their wives' incomes as pin money or as a means of making frivolous purchases.

New and liberated husbands take a more sensible (and less sexist) view of income generated by their wives. It is real money, to be integrated into the total pool of family income. New and liberated husbands agree that a wife's income has as much dignity and value as that earned by a husband.

A More Balanced View of Work

An industrial psychologist from New York University is both a new husband and a well-respected person in his field. In the preface to an important textbook he wrote, he thanked his wife and children for making all the effort necessary for putting the book together seem worthwhile. Many people say things like this, but this man meant it. He is a person destined to become prominent in his field, and yet his drive for success has not become obsessive.

Being a new husband seems to add a sense of balance toward a man's career. As I describe them, most new husbands are career oriented and yet few of them are *workaholics.* Perhaps responding to the needs of a wife and/or children serves as a brake upon total devotion to a career. Rather than detracting from success in a career, such responsiveness to a family can help a man achieve a sense of balance. Al, a key executive in the graphic arts field, makes this comment about work obsessions:

"My verdict after twenty-five years of watching executives come and go is that a work-obsessed man is a dangerous man. If I catch a man working late hours night after night, I urge him to seek help. Often the help he needs is a marriage counselor. A man who spends a weekend devoted to his family comes back to the office with a fresh outlook and a recharged battery.

"I hope I'm not being a sticky sentimentalist, but there is something more valuable about a family than a hobby for giving a man a new perspective. As I look back upon my younger days, I can legitimately say that I made better decisions on the days that I left a kitchen table full of smiling faces at home. The guy who hardly ever sees his family during the week can run stale. Maybe a person needs a little love to make sound business decisions."

Sentimentalist or not, Al has a good point. Providing for a family is not the exclusive purpose of a career, but it does add meaning to work. At least new husbands see it this way and thus reap the benefits of their perception.

Children Become Companions

New and liberated husbands reap extraordinary benefits from raising children: they acquire companionships that endure up to eighteen years and perhaps through a lifetime. Many people utter the phrase "children are great" out of social pressure, but new husbands are sincere in this utterance. By relating closely to a child or children and making an honest effort to understand his/her or their world, a new husband gets as much out of child rearing as he gives. New husbands usually enjoy doing things *with* rather than *for* their children. The difference is subtle, but substantial. Seth, a new husband

and finance professor, explains the return on emotional investment he derives from his relationship with his two children—both boys.

"Paul is thirteen and Frank is nine. I think I do a reasonable job of the parentlike things a father is supposed to do such as instilling a sense of the importance of homework, toothbrushing, not picking on animals, or making fun of physically or emotionally handicapped people. To use a leadership term, these are the control functions a parent is supposed to perform. But if that were all I did with Paul and Frank I would be missing out on a very important part of my life.

"The boys have their own friends and their own interests. When I take them to their little league games, they are there mostly with their friends. I get lost quietly on the sidelines and cheer just enough not to embarrass them. I recognize there are times when a father shouldn't dote over his children. In spite of this, there are many things the three of us do together that represent really happy times for me.

"I could cite maybe fifty little situations that would help explain the kind of relationship I have with my boys. All of the situations I have in mind illustrate the same theme. I'm their father; yet the three of us are also companions. The boys and I love police detective stories. Our favorite show is on Monday night. The three of us sit lined up on the family room couch completely enthralled with what's happening in the story. It's hard to find situations in life where you can completely relax. Aside from my wife and the boys, I can't think of any other relationship where I can leave my work concerns behind at least once in a while.

"It must be hard for you to explain to a childless adult how watching television with two children can be a peak experience in life. It's about equally difficult to explain to a childless adult that buying a minibike for a child is more fun than buying a sportscar for yourself.

"Just by being close to my children and getting involved in their world, I get a lot out of being a parent. Paul and Frank are giving me many of the good things in life without them even realizing it."

Masculine Boys, Feminine Girls

Unisex children, effeminate boys, and masculine girls are in style in some circles. Many liberated people regard the concepts of masculinity and femininity as false cultural stereotypes. Given enough time an advocate of a society free of sex roles will uncover an astounding anthropological fact such as, "In one aboriginal village a mincing walk is considered masculine, while an O.J. Simpsonlike gait is considered feminine." Definitions of masculinity and femininity are tied to specific cultures but not for indefinite time periods. However, most people relate to their present culture.

Assume a father did prefer to bring up a masculine boy and a feminine daughter without being rigid about the sexual difference. Also assume he was old-fashioned enough to take pride in rearing a masculine son and a feminine daughter. The most practical way he could influence such development of his children would be to spend considerable amounts of time with them and show them that he loved them. In addition, he would (and I can feel the wrath of radical feminists responding to this comment) relate in a slightly different way to the son from the daughter. For instance, research evidence (already cited in an earlier chapter) suggests that treating a female child like a "little lady" encourages femininity.

In short, another by-product from being a new husband is having children who are proud of their sexual identification. For many men, a by-product like this is beautiful.

Less Juvenile Delinquency

Juvenile delinquency is a complex asocial act with a number of roots. An outstandingly consistent finding, however, is that juvenile delinquents are neglected by parents, too severely disciplined by parents, or given no guidelines at all. Parents who batter children (adult delinquents), for example, were usually battered by their parents. A new husband approach to child rearing seems to be the right blend of caring and guidance to ward off the usual roots of acting out behavior that results in juvenile crime.

Joe, an almost pure strain of patriarch, was the self-appointed monitor of moral behavior in his community. He formed a citizen's decency league to bar sexually explicit movies from being shown in his town. His constant campaigning for a better community combined with his demanding job left him little time to spend with his five children. When he was home, he served as the disciplinarian and task master.

His oldest son left for college—a parochial institution of national reputation. Within three months the young man was arrested for car theft. Confused, his father lashed out at society, "I can't understand what happened to my son. Despite all the beatings I've given him for stepping out of line, he still got into trouble. But what can you expect from a society that allows women and children to see people performing sex acts on the screen?"

Next time Joe should perhaps try a new husband approach to child rearing. He should substitute involvement for moralism, and use encouragement for the right behavior rather than physical punishment for the wrong behavior.

Less Backlash at Home

A new husband is subject to a lot less backlash at home than a husband who tries to make all the decisions and avoids household responsibilities. The wives of new husbands are much less susceptible to the housewife syndrome or cabin fever—even when these women are basically full-time homemakers. As one man who converted from an old husband to a new husband commented in a group discussion about marital relationships:

"What a difference in the amount of mental anguish I'm subjected to now as compared to my past life. I joined the twentieth century and began to relate to my wife as a person and also take on regular household chores. I took the advice of my wife and started to do more with my children than two hours a week of play. Very soon thereafter much of her harping, carping, moaning, and groaning subsided.

"It hit me that much of her complaining was justified. Of course, I didn't make 100 percent of the concessions. In return for my becoming a better husband and father, my wife agreed to stop bitching about trivial things. Now that this undercurrent of ill will has disappeared in our household, I feel like I have a lot more energy left for constructive purposes."

A More Flexible Life Style

Another benefit a man might derive from being a new husband (and having a *new* wife) is that it gives him more options in life. Feeling no strong need to hold all the power and make all the money within a family unit, he builds more flexibility into his life style. Syd, a new husband and creative type, is one example of the flexible approach to living and working a new husband can enjoy.

"I was Big Syd the advertising account executive, bagging down $37,000 per year in one of Los Angeles' biggest agencies. I was doing well and perhaps headed toward a partnership in a really big, prestigious shop. But I was getting away from creative work. I began to think that my facility for entertaining people and setting up budgets was becoming more important than my ability to communicate ideas to the public. I was spending more time shuffling papers and commuting than I was doing things that could help me grow professionally.

"If I spun off from the agency that I worked for and started a conventional agency of my own, I would soon be back in the same trap. In order to look good I would need beautiful offices. In order to pay for the big overhead I would have to keep growing. That would mean I would slip back again into administrative work.

"Instead I took a page from an artist's notebook. We sold our home and bought an old house in the city. It became the base of operations for my new agency—a tiny advertising boutique. My shop was basically a one-person operation with help subcontracted for as needed. My overhead was low enough that I could afford to take on just the kind of clients I really wanted. And I could put some of my creative talent to work that was getting stale in my executive role.

"My wife took over about one-quarter of the building for something she had long wanted to do. She designed, made, and sold hanging flower pots, vases, and similar items.

"With tax write-offs on just about everything, it didn't take a heck of a lot of cash coming into our businesses to provide enough money to live well. We rented an apartment walking distance from the house. Should we hit a recession in business, we can actually live in our office. Should I decide to return to a large agency, my wife could always rent my portion of the space to a waterbed or health food store or anything like it. It's comforting to realize you have alternatives in life."

More Personal Freedom

An old husband explained to his therapist that the reason he spent so little time away from home is that he did not want to create a situation whereby his wife would be left with too much free time. By his staying home at night and avoiding business travel as much as possible, his wife wouldn't have much opportunity to commit adultery. In addition, if he discouraged her going out with her friends for dinner she would not be exposed to men in restaurants and bars. His therapist offered this insight:

"Don't you realize that by trying to limit your wife's freedom you are restricting yours? The prison guard who sits outside cells with gun in hand has about as much freedom as the person inside the cell—at least for the time the guard is on duty. The man who keeps his dog tied to the end of the leash has as much freedom to roam as the dog. The leash is connected to both the man and the dog. Oppressors don't have much more freedom than the people they are trying to oppress."

New husbands enjoy more freedom than old husbands in other aspects of their domestic lives. A new husband who encourages a wife to develop her own interests as a person is simultaneously placed in a situation where he has more freedom and time to pursue his interests. A new husband, who stays close to his children and offers them the right amount of discipline at the right time, finds that he ultimately has more freedom than his counterpart who mismanages child rearing. A father who attempts to overcontrol his children may eventually become plagued with the burden of facing the consequences of a rebellious teen-ager.

The new husband who responds to his wife's emotional needs and shares household responsibilities enjoys the freedom most married men envy—the freedom that is associated with not absorbing the complaints and grumbles (however justified) of a discontented wife.

The totally liberated husband who has lost his masculine identity in his attempt to be free from being cast into a specific role has lost some of his freedom. He is no longer free to be a strong male figure—at least in his present family situation.

An increased sense of personal freedom is a potent incentive for many men. Even potent enough to make other kinds of husbands curious about becoming new husbands.

chapter 11

Making the Switch

An old husband can become a new husband if he wants to. Although it is never easy to bring about changes in attitude and behavior, there are thoughts a man might ponder and steps he might take that could bring about the switch. Liberated husbands who want to switch back to being new husbands may have an easier time than old husbands who want to become new husbands. Most liberated husbands at one time thought and acted like new husbands.

I have developed thirty constructive suggestions for the aspiring new husband. Just the fact that a man wants to become a new husband is significant. An important first step has been taken—a self-imposed desire for change. Not every suggestion of mine will fit every potential convert. Conceivably you are already ahead of many of these suggestions. Pick and choose from among those that make the most sense to you as an individual. Even if your metamorphosis is not complete you may reap many of the benefits forthcoming from leading the life style of a new husband. At a minimum, I invite you to try out a few of these suggestions before dismissing their relevance to your particular life circumstances.

1. Before jumping ahead further in the direction of becoming a new husband, make sure that your wife is interested in having you make such a change. She may be an emotionally healthy, contented woman who has always dreamed of having an old-fashioned husband. The much maligned feminine mystique may be alive and real for her. Perhaps she needs to change more than you do. If you change and she resists having a new husband around the house, your relationship may be headed toward the rocks. Not everybody can tolerate change.

If the new husband life style is what you want and she can only feel comfortable with an old husband, it is most likely a symptom that the two of you have incompatible ideas about major aspects of daily living. See a marriage counselor, but only if you're not afraid that a full discussion of your differences could lead to a drifting apart.

2. Retake the New Husband Scale presented in Chapter 2. If your score is higher than before it could indicate that just the process of reading this book has influenced your thinking. (Caution: There is a possibility that reading this book has taught you the so-called right answers and this is why your score is now higher. This problem has plagued behavioral scientists for years.)

If your thinking has legitimately moved in the direction of becoming a new husband by the simple expedient of reading this book, you are indeed a flexible person. You should be able to make the switch from an old to a new husband with relative ease.

3. If you are serious about becoming a new husband, begin soon to improve your work habits. In order to do justice to your career, spend loads of time with your wife and children, help out around the house, and still have some time for yourself, you will have to be well organized. If you are a procrastinator (like most people—even some successful ones), you may not be able to hack being a new husband.

If it takes you all Saturday morning to get caught up on your office paper work, you are going to miss out on a lot of little league games your sons and daughters might have scheduled. Without being well organized you may not have time to cook dinner, bathe the baby, wash the dog, and still get that crash project finished your boss wants by nine tomorrow morning.

4. If your wife and children regard you as a strong male figure, accept it with grace, and consider it a compliment. Being a strong male figure is not incompatible with being sensitive and gentle toward people you care about. Despite some rumbles to the contrary in recent years, there is nothing inherently wrong in being *masculine.*

5. Join a male consciousness raising group. It should help sensitize you to the fact that many males have legitimate gripes about the demands society places upon them. Despite the legitimacy of these gripes and feelings, it may not be to your advantage to capitulate to the totally liberated male side. You'll miss out on a lot of the fun a new husband gets out of taking care of his many responsibilities. It's usually more fun to have people dependent upon you than for you to be dependent upon them. Ask anybody who is out of a job.

6. Arrange your home situation with your wife so she gets an occasional night off from the routine of staying home with you and/or the children. Only the most suspicious of old husbands hold their wives accountable for every minute they spend outside the house (aside from working, shopping, or spending time with the children).

7. At the same time arrange things with your wife so there is room in the household schedule for you to have personal time off. A potential danger in being a caring, sharing, loving husband and father is that there will be no time left over for your personal enjoyment away from the family or job. Personal time off will help you maintain a fresh perspective.

8. You cannot be a new husband without making some contribution to housekeeping. Divide up home-making tasks, perhaps on a rotating basis, with your wife (and children if they are old enough). Every couple has to work out for themselves what is the most sensible distribution of chores. The man may prefer garage cleaning to sewing buttons back on garments or vice versa. Don't divide up the tasks along rigid ideas of male versus female chores.

In general the person who works the larger number of hours outside the home, or who has less physical energy because of outside work, should be required to spend the lesser amount of time doing housework. However, the entire sharing system will break down if the husband performs no household chores, even if the wife is a full-time homemaker.

9. Prepare a meal inside the home (or use the yard or balcony) for your wife at least once a month. If you hate fancy cooking, cook for yourself and children on your wife's night out. Children delight in having their father prepare them a meal.

10. At a minimum, make sure you develop enough skill in the kitchen whereby you are not dependent upon somebody else to prepare you a meal. Nobody is less free than somebody who has to depend upon other people to get him or her through the routine of daily living. Only invalids and infants should be absolutely dependent upon another individual for essential housekeeping tasks. *Choosing* to have these services performed for you, however, may be a sign of good judgment.

11. Find some activity other than dining and sex that you and your wife can perform together on a relatively equal level (perhaps scuba diving, dancing, skiing, or antiquing). Use this joint activity as a supplement to the individual interests the two of you may have been developing all your lives.

12. Conduct a discussion session with your wife about the future plans you both have. Perhaps you and she have similar thoughts about the future. Perhaps she is looking toward a simpler, less materialistic life than you are. Maybe she has plans to spend money way beyond your capacity to earn it. Whatever your hopes and plans, the few couples I have observed share their futures became a more unified team in the process. You might even find that some compromise about your futures will be necessary to arrive at a life plan that works for both of you.

13. Figure out if you and your wife are engaging in dialogues or monologues. Ask her what she hears you saying the next time you have a heavy discussion. Then you tell her what you hear her saying. Next, both of you comment whether or not the other person does see your point of view. If you're not getting across your point of view to each other, you are engaging in monologue, not dialogue. To illustrate, here is a brief bit of dialogue:

HE: "Gloria, I learned today that the average American family of four can live moderately well on about $13,000 per year. Our family income is $4000 higher than that."

SHE: "That is something, isn't it?"

HE: "Gloria, what am I trying to tell you?"

SHE: "Vance, you're telling me that we should be doing well because we make a little more than the average American family."

HE: "That's exactly what I'm trying to tell you, but I can tell from the tone of your voice and your facial expression that you have a different interpretation."

SHE: "How perceptive you are. I think that a graduate engineer like yourself should be doing a helluva lot better than the average American family who is just getting by."

14. Strike from your conscious mind the idea that you are baby-sitting when you are taking care of your young children. You are not baby-sitting any more than your wife is baby-sitting when she takes care of the child. Are you "wife-sitting" when you do things with your wife? Is she "husband-sitting" when she entertains you? Baby-sitting is for people who get paid small sums of money to take care of other people's children. Pity the child whose father baby-sits for him or her.

15. Ask your children for suggestions on how you and they (or just him or her) might have more fun together as a group. As one eight-year-old girl told her father (who believed that children only had fun in structured activities), "Let's just goof around and do nothing together." Children shouldn't call all the shots but they often have some solid ideas about fun.

16. Encourage flexible attitudes in your children about male and female roles, but don't discourage a boy from developing masculine interests and a girl from developing feminine interests. For instance, you might tell your daughter that both boys and girls take ballet lessons and that girls can compete on the same teams with boys in high school. However, should your three-year-old daughter want a toy oven and a Barbie Doll for Christmas, don't buy her a football and a toy automobile service station instead. If your four-year-old son begs for a cowboy holster and gun set, don't substitute a toy ironing board set and call him a sexist.

17. Search for a new job, or perhaps a new field, if your present job situation is so oppressive you have no time or energy left over to become a new husband (or even a good, old one). Jobs with unrealistic demands have wrecked many home situations. It is not unknown for a man seemingly locked into such a job to find a new job that pays more, is more exciting, and yet simultaneously gives him more time to get involved with his family. A bad job is only a temporary excuse for postponing becoming a new husband.

18. Reserve your right to earn a high income, and advance in your career. However, should your wife and children feel awkward when you are home at night during the middle of the week, your quest for career advancement may have gone too far. Being a new husband requires a delicate balancing act between career and family.

19. Given a choice about relocation, make it a major family decision involving the preferences of your wife and adolescent or teenage children. Your opinion and preferences should be given equal, if not greater weight, but a group decision is crucial about dramatic changes in a family's life situation. Nevertheless, there are times when relocation is your only alternative to unemployment. Under those circumstances, do the best you can to help your family manage the inevitable inconveniences. Many families, in fact, thrive on relocation even when the prospects appear gloomy.

20. Find a way to get your wife and children involved in your work. If you work as a systems interface analyst, for example, and your wife doesn't know what that entails (and you understand yourself), explain it to her. Take family members to the office and explain the relevance of your work to them. It's easier to be a new husband to a wife who understands and cares about the nature of your work, than to be one to a woman who has no concern about your occupation. It's also easier to be a new husband type of father toward children who think your work is important than to relate this way to children who don't care what you do for a living.

21. Do not attempt to decide for your wife what life style you feel would be the best for her. Whether or not your wife wants to be a full-time homemaker is *her* decision. This does not mean that your preferences should not influence her decision. Likewise her preferences should influence what life style you choose. Wouldn't it be difficult to be a full-time househusband without your wife's emotional (and financial) support?

22. Listen with sympathy to your wife's or girlfriend's complaints about her role in life. Until you help the woman you live with find a role in life she finds at least satisfactory, it is difficult to be a new husband. To reverse the situation, no matter how much your wife would try to respond to your needs and do things with and for you, it would not compensate for the fact that you disliked the breadwinner role. Conceivably your career-minded wife now wants to begin raising a family; or your family-minded wife now wants to start building a career. Maybe she would prefer that you became a working househusband. At least give it a thought.

23. Encourage almost anything your wife might want to do in terms of personal development. The best way to show concern about another individual is to help that person grow. Perhaps you are not in a financial position to send your wife to medical school (as one new husband is doing) but you can help her decide upon a plan of action for personal and professional growth. An implicit mutual understanding many successful couples have is "You help me grow, and I'll help you grow."

24. Talk out feelings of competition and rivalry you and your wife might have. A new husband has the edge over an old husband with respect to recognizing that any two people living together inevitably develop some feelings of rivalry and competition. If you envy her success in her work, talk about it. If she envys your ranking on the squash ladder at your club, talk about that too. Rivalry and competition that is suppressed may cause as many problems in a marriage as concerns about sex or money.

25. Develop your own equitable way of sharing expenses if you and your wife both work. A simple system of "who pays for what" is much better than the complexities of pooling income and then breaking down a prorated expense analysis for every purchase. For instance you might pay for vacations and she pay for furniture. It beats standing in the hotel lobby at the end of a vacation dividing up the hotel bill in this manner: "You ordered the room service lunch, I called home, you charged horseback riding. . . ." In general, expenses should be shared according to ability to pay. Some expenses logically belong to him (for example, alimony, child support, vasectomy) while some expenses belong logically to her (clothing for herself, sports lessons, hysterectomy). Happy income sharing. Money is a very emotional topic.

26. Work hard to earn more money than your wife does, but don't regard it as a loss of masculinity if your wife pulls ahead financially. Now that many artificial barriers have been lifted against the progress of women in business, a goodly number of women whose talent and drives exceed those of their husbands will surpass them in income.

27. Develop an encouraging and supportive attitude

toward the occasional business trips your wife might take. A woman who is out of town is not necessarily more likely to have an affair, be mugged, beaten, raped, robbed, or missing in action than a woman who never leaves town. Your own town may have a higher crime rate than you realize.

28. Try at least a brief stint at being a housespouse (the latest word for homemaker). It will develop your domestic skills, thus enabling you to function more effectively as a new husband. You might be able to achieve the same results by working home on occasion. Join the legion of a growing number of people in many fields who sometimes work at home to take care of various kinds of paper work or to do some creative thinking. Driving to the office is expensive, time consuming, and quite often inefficient. Any work done at home rather than in the office is thus to the good.

29. Make sexology at least a minor hobby. Every general bookstore stocks useful books about developing your sex technique. By all means involve your wife in your quest for improvement in this area. To fully qualify as a new husband you and your wife or girlfriend have to communicate emotionally and physically in bed. (Disregard sexpertise as a new husband requirement if you and your woman don't care much for sex. About 5 percent of the people are really asexual.)

30. Be enthusiastic about your new husband life style if you make the switch. However, think of new husbandry in realistic terms. No single life style can guarantee happiness at home and productivity at work for everyone, although being a new husband certainly can help.

Notes

Chapter 3

1. Betty Yorburg, *The Changing Family,* New York: Columbia University Press, 1973, p. 200.

2. Andrew J. DuBrin, *Survival in the Sexist Jungle,* Chatsworth, California: Books for Better Living, 1974, p. 164.

Chapter 5

1. Lawrence H. Fuchs, *Family Matters,* New York: Random House, 1972, p. 201.

2. *Ibid.,* p. 202.

3. Bruno Bettelheim, "The Roots of Radicalism," *Playboy,* March 1971. Reprinted in *Annual Editions: Readings in Human Development* '73–'74, Guilford, Connecticut: Dushkin Publish Group, 1973, p. 217.

4. Henry B. Biller, *Father, Child, and Sex Role: Paternal Determinants of Personality Development,* Lexington, Mass.: Heath Lexington Books, 1971, p. 9.

5. *Ibid.,* p. 33.

6. *Ibid.,* p. 73.

7. *Ibid.,* p. 118.

Chapter 6

1. Stella B. Jones, "Geographic Mobility as Seen by the Wife and Mother," *Journal of Marriage and the Family,* May 1973, p. 216.

2. Andrew J. DuBrin, *Women in Transition,* Springfield, Illinois: Charles C Thomas, 1972, pp. 47–48.

Chapter 7

1. Lynda Lytle Holmstrom, *The Two-Career Family,* Cambridge, Mass.: Schenkman Publishing Company, 1972, p. 113.

2. *Ibid.,* p. 114.

3. *Ibid.,* p. 92.

4. Mary Margaret Bothwell, "The Growing Trend Toward Weekend Marriages," *New Woman,* January-February, 1974, pp. 73, 75.

5. *Ibid.,* p. 75.

Chapter 8

1. "He Quit Job to be 'Househusband,'" *Rochester Democrat and Chronicle,* January 25, 1974, p. 2C.

2. Liz Roman Gallese, "The Nonworkers: Joe Errera Finds Being Fulltime Homemaker is Rewarding Experience," *Wall Street Journal,* March 16, 1973, pp. 1, 12.

3. Mary Rita Kurycki, "Making Role-Playing Work in a Modern Marriage," *Rochester Democrat and Chronicle,* September 15, 1974, pp. 1E, 8E.

Chapter 9

1. Harry Nelson, "Plastic Device Used to Solve Impotence," (D&C—Los Angeles Times) *Rochester Democrat and Chronicle,* September 16, 1973, p. 10E.

2. Irving London, "Frigidity, Sensitivity, and Sexual Roles," in Joseph H. Pleck and Jack Sawyer (editors), *Men*

and Masculinity, Englewood Cliffs, N.J.: A Spectrum Book, 1974, p. 41.

3. Albert Ellis, "Healthy and Disturbed Reasons for Having Extramarital Relations," in Gerhard Neubeck and Vera M. Schletzer (editors), *Extramarital Relations,* Englewood Cliffs, N.J.: Prentice-Hall, 1969, p. 159.

Index